T0103938

TRANSFORMING *Moments* WITH GOD

Ninety Devotions to Strengthen Your Relationship with God

FRANK KING

All Scriptures taken from the King James Version of the Bible unless otherwise noted

WestBow Press books may be ordered through booksellers or by contacting:

WestBow Press
A Division of Thomas Nelson & Zondervan
1663 Liberty Drive
Bloomington, IN 47403
www.westbowpress.com
1 (866) 928-1240

ISBN: 978-1-4908-9099-9 (sc)
ISBN: 978-1-4908-9100-2 (hc)
ISBN: 978-1-5127-1477-7 (e)

Print information available on the last page.

WestBow Press rev. date: 10/27/2015

Contents

Preface

Why should we value our time alone with God? Because it is the means by which we enter His awesome presence. Yes, the same One who created the heavens, the earth, the sea, and everything that is in them. Time with Him can set or change the climate of our entire day. Through our communion with Him, battles can be won even before they manifest themselves.

But many of us find ourselves trying to juggle too many balls in the air of life. We have increasingly more to do within the same limited time. We must not allow the busyness of life to prevent us from communing daily with the Father, however. If we do, we assure ourselves of a life that is mediocre at best, relative to the life He has called us to live.

Transforming Moments with God can be effectively used in as little as ten minutes a day. In three months, your relationship with Him can be greatly strengthened, or even revolutionized. The key Scripture in each devotion was carefully chosen during a span of several months as I sought verses most suited for the cause.

This book of devotions is not intended to replace your personal Bible study time. So let me tell you how I envision this book being used. The most effective time to use it, I believe, is early in the morning to begin your day and to set the climate for the remainder of the day. It can also be used at lunch time. But this will be effective only if a secluded place void of interruptions is available. Thirdly, this book can be used at night as a time of refreshing after a long day.

Another important point is that this is a book of devotions and not a regular book. It's not to be just read through. It is to be experienced, one devotion per day, until the book has been completed.

I found my inspiration for this book in 2 Corinthians 3:18. It says, "But we all, with open face beholding as in a glass the glory of the Lord, are changed into the same image from glory to glory, even as by the Spirit of the Lord." That is, as we behold the Lord's glory—as reflected in the Scriptures--we are progressively transformed into the likeness of that same glory by the work of the Holy Spirit!

Think about it. That's exactly what should be happening in church when we come to hear the Word of God. That is, a preacher whom God has called expounds on the Scriptures so we can plainly see the glory in the text. And from week to week the Holy Spirit changes us into the likeness of that glory.

As a pastor, I've seen that process at work. It goes something like this: Someone accepts Christ and is passionate for Him. Every Sunday and Wednesday the person comes to church, hungry for the Word of God. As he gets a regular diet of sound doctrine and beholds the glory in the Scriptures, the Holy Spirit progressively transforms him into the Lord's likeness. With time, the person becomes a giant for Christ and can teach others. I can't explain how it all happens. This is the Lord's doing, and it is marvelous in our eyes.

Each devotion in this book includes what I call a meditational thought. This is a thought-provoking point designed to help the reader experience the truth at hand more deeply. Each thought is a message in and of itself. Oftentimes, the wisdom in the thought is not readily apparent. Those who take a minute and meditate on these nuggets will find the spiritual gold.

Following each meditational thought, a couple of lines have been provided for personal reflection on the devotion. Simply jot down a thought that comes to you as a result of the devotion.

Finally, each devotion in this book ends with the beginning of a prayer. *Beginning* I say because the intent is that the reader will finish the prayer with what's in his own heart. The concept of "praying the

Word back to God" is so powerful. When we do that, we can be confident we are praying according to His will. I have made this practice a part of my personal Bible study time over the past decade or more. It may be a single thought or concept that seemed to come alive during my study time. My doing this enables me to talk to God about something He has just spoken to me about through His Word.

I firmly believe that the verses I have chosen to address in this book of devotions are some of the most powerful ones in the entire Bible. I have labored to share with simplicity some of what the Lord has shown me in those Scriptures. My prayer is that as you use this book to spend moments with God that you will see His glory in the text. Moreover, through the work of the Holy Spirit, you will be progressively changed from glory to glory.

Acknowledgments

Praises be to the God of my salvation and to Christ my Savior. I feel so honored to be entrusted with the grace to minister to people from all walks of life through the spoken and written Word. I especially dedicate this book to the people of God who make sacred their time alone with Him. This one is for you. To those who have been so gracious in supporting my writing ministry in the past, I say a big God bless you. Last but not least, I truly thank God for my lovely wife Cynthia, and for our six wonderful children, Tyneise, Candice, Sharice, Frank, Timothy, and Stefan.

1. God Visits Us

When I consider your heavens, the work of your fingers, the moon and the stars, which you have ordained; What is man, that you are mindful of him? and the son of man that you visit him? (Psalm 8:3-4)

Think about some of the most famous people in the world whom you admire. What do you think would happen if you were to call one of them—that's if you could get a valid phone number—and request a meeting? Most likely, though you may have bought all of the person's CDs, or gone to all of his professional games, or gone to see all of her movies, your request would not be granted. Such a person is just too big and famous to see about little you.

On the other hand, we can talk to God whenever we want to. Lest there be any misunderstanding, I am talking about the omnipresent, omniscient, omnipotent God of all creations, the Potentate and Judge of all the earth. By His wisdom He makes all things good, and His ways are past finding out. Why would such an awesome God visit us and pay any attention to us when we pray? The proclamation very clearly stated in the psalmist's question is that God does visit us through prayer.

This wonder—that is, that the Creator of the universe communes with mortal men—can be intimidating. To some, it is unthinkable to expect the God of the heavens to hear them and to respond to their petitions. Hence, they go through a religious exercise of prayer, not expecting anything to ensue, which guarantees them that nothing will.

Prayer was not our idea but God's. He has not presented it as an option but a mandate for His people. Clearly, He wants to commune with us. At least three facts reside in this truth. One, God highly values our relationship with Him. Two, He is interested in what we have to say. Thirdly, prayer ushers us into His presence.

We cannot fathom the depth of God's desire to fellowship with us. How it must displease Him when we fail to spend time with Him. His throne is in heaven, a distance too far from earth to measure. Through prayer, however, He personally visits us—every time we want it to be so, and as long as we want Him to. And this was His idea, not ours.

MEDITATIONAL THOUGHT: *God can't resist a good prayer meeting*

Personal reflection: ________________________________

____

Prayer:

Dear God in Heaven. Thank You for the awesome gift of prayer. When I consider the works of Your hands, who am I that You are here with me? I stand in awe of Your presence. I know that You hear my prayers .... Amen.

2. Trusting God

Then God said, "Take your son, your only son, Isaac, whom you love, and go to the region of Moriah. Sacrifice him there as a burnt offering on one of the mountains I will tell you about" (Genesis 22:2, NIV)

God's ways seldom appeal to logic. Sometimes He calls us to a hard thing with little details. So it was that He called old man Abraham to go to an unspecified location to offer up as a burnt offering his only son Isaac. This means Isaac would be consumed by fire.

How could God the Creator of life require a man to sacrifice his only son to Him by fire? There is but one way for a person to obey such a calling with peace. It's called trust. If what we plan to do for God must make sense before we proceed, we will accomplish little for Him.

Those who have been called to do great works for the Lord and have answered that call have testimonies that challenge conventional wisdom. God does not operate in the safe zone. He seldom calls us to do what's comfortable. This was true of Him in days of old. It is still true today—even in these uncertain times.

Trust is a necessity of life. Every day, millions travel bridges spanning wide rivers such that if the bridge failed it would be fatal. Travelers trust the authorities' assessment that such bridges are safe to cross, and so they do. Most of the many travelers who board airplanes have no idea of how they work, but they frequent them trusting that they will arrive safely to their destinations. Patients trust their physicians to put them to sleep and remove portions of their body, expecting to be better when it's all over.

Our trust in God should surpass our trust in all of these.

A vast contrast is noted. We can see the bridge, and we know people who safely cross it daily. The similar is true about flying on planes and people submitting to surgeons. But God is invisible. His primary way of speaking to us is not through an audible voice but through the Bible. Plus, it is possible that the area in which we are being called to obey Him is a place we have never been before.

To have any stability in our relationship with God we must learn to trust Him. That does not require us to completely understand His instructions or commandments. On the contrary, trust is required because many times what God is asking us to do won't make any sense to us.

MEDITATIONAL THOUGHT: *Trust trumps understanding*

Personal reflection: ______________________________

____

Prayer:

Dear Lord, I want to grow in my relationship with You so I can trust Your Word and obey Your voice, no matter what the charge. Please forgive me for those times during which I failed to trust You. Help me to trust You more…Amen.

3. Power to Serve

And, behold, I send the promise of my Father upon you: but tarry ye in the city of Jerusalem, until ye be endued with power from on high (Luke 24:49).

Our culture vastly differs from that of our forefathers. The world is a much more complex place. Sexual immorality is rampant. Many of the crimes making the news today were once unthinkable. It appears that no measure implemented by authorities can significantly stem the tide. The church struggles to be relevant.

The Lord wants to do more than save us just to attend church and enjoy Him while the world remains in darkness. Our current culture has not caught Him by surprise. He even knows the state the world will be in at His return, whenever that is. He has provided us power to serve this generation. It is the same power He clothed His apostles with almost 2000 years ago.

We read about that power at work in their lives in the book of the Acts of the Apostles after the day of Pentecost. They met much opposition after Christ left them behind to spread the gospel. Because He had equipped them through the power of the Holy Spirit, however, they accomplished their mission.

The power available to us is greater than any other power on earth. Not that this is without significance. For we fight against more than flesh and blood. If that were the only culprit, our law enforcement agencies would have a better handle on the problem than they currently do. The main criminal running rampart in our world is the devil. The result is spiritual wickedness. That's the source behind many of the heinous crimes we hear about in the news. All the latest technologies available to us in our highly advanced society are totally powerless against spiritual wickedness. But God has given us the Holy Spirit. Through this power, He makes us extraordinary in our service to Him. The Holy Spirit gives us authority in the spiritual realm, the place where the weapons of men have no effect.

This current era can become the church's greatest hour. God has not called us to cower in a corner somewhere because of this wicked world. We must do more than beg Christ to return so we can escape this earth. The church is the only hope for this dying world. God wants to use us for His glory. He has equipped us with the needed power. In these last days He has poured out His Spirit to supernaturally empower the church.

MEDITATIONAL THOUGHT: *Power from heaven is not an option but a must*

Personal reflection: ________________________________

____

Prayer:

Dear Lord, I thank You that the enemy has no power over me. The power at work in my life is greater than the powers at work in this world. Teach me how to yield myself more completely to the work of the Spirit in my service to you…Amen.

4. Faith versus Circumstances

And Simon answering said unto him, Master, we have toiled all the night, and have taken nothing: nevertheless at thy word I will let down the net (Luke 5:5)

What do you do when you are highly skilled in a particular area and based on your circumstances, God's instructions to you seem illogical? Being a self-proclaimed expert in the field, you may feel qualified to contend with God. We must arrive at the point where we exalt His words above all else.

Peter the disciple was a fisherman. He knew how to fish. He had toiled all night long and had caught absolutely nothing. He washed his net and was ready to call it quits. Then Jesus showed up and instructed him to let down his net for a catch. This must have really challenged Peter. He was not a novice. He was a fisherman. He knew the waters. The fish were not biting. Nevertheless, he obeyed the Lord and great was his catch!

How often have we clearly heard what the Lord instructed us to do, but we chose to walk by sight and not by faith in His Word? It seemed reasonable. After all, we can see reality—at least what appears to be reality. This tends to have a more profound impact on our senses than something that's intangible, such as our faith in God and His Word.

In every situation in life there are at least two sources that speak to us. One is our circumstances. In adversity they remind us of the desperation of our moment. They tempt us to act unwisely. The other source is the Word of God. It calls us to focus on and trust Him. Our life must march to the drum beat of the latter. This must be true even in situations in which we consider ourselves to be a subject matter expert, we have already made our assessment, and the Lord's counsel runs counter to our verdict. May we say as Peter said, "Nevertheless, at Your Word."

We tend to be OK with "trusting God's Word" when the stakes are not too high. That way if He doesn't come through, the loss we suffer will be little or none. Or, if He doesn't act by our imposed deadline, our contingency plan can be implemented thereby redeeming the time we "lost" waiting on Him. But this is not the place where God operates. He calls us to trust Him completely—when everything around us says otherwise.

MEDITATIONAL THOUGHT: *Faith defies logic*

Personal reflection: ______________________________

____

Prayer:

Dear God, I want to walk in a new level of trusting You. When Your Word speaks to me, may it influence me more than my circumstances do. Even when doubters mock my trust, help me to embrace Your Word wholeheartedly…Amen.

5. No Fear of Death

And deliver them who through fear of death were all their lifetime subject to bondage (Hebrew 2:15)

You can find many books on what foods you should eat to keep you looking younger longer. Some people go under the knife to hide the effects of aging. We keep searching for but have not found the fountain of youth. The bottom line is that death is certain for all of us if the Lord tarries long enough.

Having only one life to live, some people are preoccupied with the thought of death. Some go as far as evaluating every adventure in life in terms of the probability of dying in the process. I have heard it said that fearful people live longer, the apparent point being that they minimize risks. Taking precautions in life has its place. But excessive fear about death is not liberty but bondage, robbing you of your quality of life.

The thought of death becomes more profound with age. In preparation for its arrival, we add to our shopping list the search for a plot at the cemetery. We make our will to designate the heirs of our possessions we will leave behind. Increasing health problems, unique to the aging, intimate that our pilgrimage is winding down.

It is natural for us to have some fear of death. It is the unknown. We have no way of infiltrating its camp, and finding out what it's all about. No one who has departed this life can come back to us and allay our anxieties.

Salvation through Christ should radically change our outlook on death, however. Before knowing Him, our life was confined to the days between the present and the grave. We viewed everything within this window. After Christ, however, the grave takes on new meaning. It is not the end but a rite of passage into eternity. These current days are no longer the best years of our existence but the life to come is.

What are the few days of this pilgrimage compared to eternity? Christ has redeemed us from the curse of the law. Hallelujah! Death has no more power to torment us. The same power that raised Christ from the dead shall also raise our mortal bodies. The earnest of this hope is the Spirit of Christ who now lives in us.

MEDITATIONAL THOUGHT: *Fear binds the otherwise free*

Personal reflection: ______________________________

____

Prayer:

Dear Lord. Thank You for the gift of eternal life. I will no longer be preoccupied with the fear of death. For to die is not lost to me but gain. I hereby declare war on all unhealthy fears in my life...Amen.

6. Another Comforter

And I will pray the Father, and he shall give you another Comforter, that he may abide with you forever (John 14:16)

Imagine being able to walk with Jesus on earth as His disciples did. You would have the benefits of His awesome counsel at any time. You would know you were never alone. When you pray, you would never doubt if He heard you.

That very kind of relationship is available to us today. Christ has returned to the Father, but at the same time He has come back to us. This He did through the person of the Holy Spirit. Jesus refers to the Holy Spirit as another Comforter. The key word here is *another*. The Greek word used here refers to another of the same kind, as opposed to another of a different kind. When Jesus told His disciples that this Comforter would be just like Him, they could relate to what Christ was saying. They had spent several years with Him. They had a good idea of what it meant to be just like Him.

Oftentimes, we are guilty of not regarding the Holy Spirit as a person. And not just any person, but the Holy Spirit is Christ living on the inside of us. Yes, the same Christ who came down from heaven to redeem us and to teach us. The same Christ who worked miracles, and exercised authority over demons.

The Bible says some awesome things about the Holy Spirit. Jesus refers to Him as the Comforter. But also, He makes intercession for us, guides us into all truth, convicts the world of sin, etc.

We must learn to hear the "voice" of the Comforter. This we will do if we spend ample time with Him. When we do that and also obey

Him, we will know what it means to be led by the Spirit. And for all practical purposes, this will constitute walking with Jesus on earth as His disciples did.

There is not a more dynamic life we can live than one characterized by vibrant fellowship with Christ through the person of the Holy Spirit. To find this place in life is to know the Comforter. The word rendering *Comforter* is one that refers to a person whom we have called alongside us. The Holy Spirit wants an invitation to occupy that place in our life.

MEDITATIONAL THOUGHT: *Christ left us to get closer to us*

Personal reflection: ____________________________

____

Prayer:

Dear Lord, Thank You for sending me the Comforter. He is the same person as Christ who walked this earth. Today, I choose to live as one accompanied by a most capable Friend walking alongside him ...Amen.

7. God's Faithfulness

Look at the birds of the air; they do not sow or reap or store away in barns, and yet your heavenly Father feeds them. Are you not much more valuable than they? (Matthew 6:26, NIV)

Countless birds fly gracefully through the air. God faithfully provides food for every one of them daily. If He does that for them, how much more will He do to provide for us who were made in His very image? That was Jesus' teaching to His disciples. He commanded them to be anxious for nothing.

If we were to grade ourselves on obeying this commandment, how would we score? It's natural to feel anxiety when we lack the basic necessities of life such as food, clothing, and shelter, and we do not have the means to meet those needs. People can do desperate things under these conditions. During the Katrina disaster, for instance, some of the New Orleans residents who refused to evacuate resorted to looting local stores that had been boarded up. They even defied authorities who watched.

Sustenance is a major concern in life for us. It's one of the motivations for an employee to go to work everyday to a job he hates. It's why customers brave long lines at the grocery store week after week. It's one reason why immigrants, legal and illegal, head for America pursuing their dream. It's one of the reasons why our government and local churches involve themselves in help ministries.

The cost of living continues to rise while our country's economic engine runs sluggishly. Politicians know how to exploit the anxiety of the people, promising them the world during their campaign. But our hope must be in the Lord who created the heavens, the earth, and everything therein. Just as He provides for the birds in the air He will provide for His children. For what Father will not provide for His own?

Jesus calls us to have faith in God's faithfulness, but there are varying degrees of such faith. The more we grow in our faith, the less we will be moved by the signs of the times. It is only when anxiety gives way to a bold confidence about life that we have come to the place commended by Christ.

Preoccupation with our temporal needs should not be our main focus in life. Rather, we must be about the Father's business. Jesus Christ perfectly modeled this before us while on earth. When we take care of God's business He takes care of us.

MEDITATIONAL THOUGHT: *Where faith lives, anxiety dies*

Personal reflection: ______________________________

____

Prayer:

Dear Lord, Great is Your faithfulness. Though You use many vehicles to supply my needs, You are ultimately my Provider. You never fail to remember me. I hereby renounce any anxieties I have about the needs in my life...Amen.

8. A New Creation

If any man be in Christ, he is a new creature: old things are passed away; behold, all things are become new (2 Corinthians 5:17)

On the seventh day, God rested from His work. But the truth is that He continues to make new creations. For He makes anew everyone who comes to Him through faith in His Son.

This truth is not without significance. For how else can we walk with God? His ways are so much higher than ours. His interests are worlds apart from our own. The difference between Him and us is immeasurable. It is on the order of this disparity that we must be changed that we might have fellowship with Him!

The idea of being made a new creation is a mystery to the unbeliever. The depth of the change is unfathomable. But all genuine believers personally know this mystery.

Not one of us was born right but everyone was born wrong—wrong with God. A new creation is the rite of passage into His family.

Once we become a new creation, God deals with us not based on who we were but who we have become. To Him, old things have passed away. All things have become new.

Some Christians still wrestle with their identity. Though they are a new creation, their old man sometimes raises its ugly head. To them, this irony may suggest that the new creation has not occurred—at least not completely. And human tendency is for us to be more driven by how we feel than by what the holy record says is truth.

Moreover, some people in this world may be bent on keeping you mired in your past. People won't let you forget the dark times of your old life. To them you look the same on the outside. As for what God has done on the inside of you, those things they cannot see.

But God does not receive the testimonies of men. Nor does our own sense of inadequacies change the verdict. He says we are a new creation, and He cannot lie. Being the doer of the work He needs no man's input. He makes all things new. As He did in the beginning of creation so He does now: And God saw that it was good.

MEDITATIONAL THOUGHT: *We were not repaired but made anew*

Personal reflection: ______________________________

____

Prayer:

Dear Lord, Thank You for radically changing my life. I know I am a new creation. Because of that I can have fellowship with You. In those areas where I still look or act like the old person I used to be, help me to live like the new creation You have made me to become.... Amen.

9. Our High Priest

For we have not an high priest which cannot be touched with the feeling of our infirmities; but was in all points tempted like as we are, yet without sin. Let us therefore come boldly unto the throne of grace, that we may obtain mercy, and find grace to help in time of need. (Hebrew 4:15-16)

In the Old Testament, the priest entered the holiest of holies before God on behalf of the people. Jesus Christ is our New Testament High Priest. He resides in glory with the Father, abiding in His presence, acting on our behalf.

Jesus is highly qualified for this role. He came down on earth and lived among men, being tempted in every area in which we are. Through it all He never sinned. He knows what it takes to live in an ungodly world while remaining perfectly faithful to God. Had He not come down on earth and lived as a human being, He would still know all things because He is omniscient. But He would not have been able to personally identify with our struggles down here.

Consider an employee who worked himself through the ranks to ultimately become the company's CEO. Now think about a son who's never worked for the company but was given the CEO's position because his dad was the company's owner. The latter would tend to not make a good leader. He would have no way of relating to what it's like being an employee. Only the former employee could be a real champion for the people, having been where they are.

So it is that Jesus, having lived on earth and having been tempted on all points as we are, is highly qualified to be our High Priest. He understands what it takes to live victoriously in this world. That's why we can come boldly to Him for help in the time of need.

We are in good hands because Jesus is the Author and the Finisher of our faith. He came on earth and humbled Himself before the cross, thereby saving us from sin. He lived the life of a servant, showing us how to live for God. And now He resides at the throne of grace, ready, willing, and able to help us in our times of need.

MEDITATIONAL THOUGHT: *Empathy breeds understanding*

Personal reflection: ______________________________

____

Prayer:

Dear Jesus, thank You for coming on earth to experience my human struggles. You are more than qualified to understand what I am going through and to plead my cause before the Father. I will come boldly to Your throne during my times of need... Amen

10. Always Triumphant

Now thanks be unto God, which always causeth us to triumph in Christ.... (2 Corinthians 2:14)

If our faith endures, we always win in Christ. We may not win every round of battle, but we will win the war. Imagine what our life would be like if this conviction became the fuel that drove us daily? Most of us have had those times when failure was imminent—or so we thought. Believing it to be so, we felt drained of energy. Too, the fight in us waned. The point is that what we believe about our fate has bearing on how we face a challenge. Hence, the question posed above.

The reason we always win in Christ is because God *causes* us to triumph. That means His hand is at work bringing victory to pass. What is the enemy against us when the Lord is actively for us?

Sometimes God allows us to go through a test that is so long and difficult we can't begin to see the end of it. We tend to get that intimidating feeling of having no idea of how things will turn out. We may feel as if we have ended up on a distant road in the middle of nowhere, after which a terrible storm suddenly arose, followed by the local power going out, resulting in utter darkness and a feeling of helplessness.

We don't always handle such times like a pro. The entire experience may go something like this: The personal trial comes, and with time our usual boldness gives way to uneasiness. A disturbed spirit replaces our inner peace. Sometimes, even bitterness toward God arises. Nevertheless, with time, He causes us to triumph. In the end, we have to repent to Him for not handling the storm better than we did.

The message in such an instance of instability is that we were not confident that in Christ we always win. For this failure to walk in faith, we need not be ashamed. We were not born with such resolve. Hence, it is not as if we have violated human nature. On the contrary, the problem is that we remained true to our humanity.

But if we truly believe that the Lord works on our behalf, causing us to always triumph, that conviction will make all the difference in our attitude during a test—if we really believe God does that for us.

MEDITATIONAL THOUGHT: *We will lose only if we fight God hard enough*

Personal reflection: ______________________________

____

Prayer:

Dear Lord, during difficult periods in my life, I know it's never Your will for me to entertain defeat. Today, I open my heart to the truth of this devotion. Strengthen my inner being so that I always expect victory no matter what the test is.... Amen.

11. Comforted to Comfort

the God of all comfort; Who comforteth us in all our tribulation, that we may be able to comfort them which are in any trouble, by the comfort wherewith we ourselves are comforted of God (2 Corinthians 1:3b, 4).

All Christians know suffering, even the most righteous. There is no predicting the length or severity of a test. Neither can we know the mind of God in terms of which particular test He will suffer us to bear. May we find consolation in this one thing—that God is the Lord of all our comfort.

His objective goes beyond simply allowing a test in our life only to turn around and comfort us. Rather, the comfort we receive from Him should become a tool of comforting others. This objective is not without significance. There is no shortage of those in this world who need to be comforted.

Anyone can apply a bandage to a wound. But those who have personally experienced the same kind of wound in question can do a much better job ministering to the wounded. For instance, there are some Christians who have known the alcohol bottle and its pain and humiliation. Through trusting God, they have obtained victory. These can minister to an alcoholic much more effectively than a person can whose life has never been touched by alcoholism. This same truth applies to our comforting the troubled.

But how quickly we forget! For s-o-o-o-n after we have gone through our ordeal and overcome, we tend to act as though we can't understand how someone else can have such a hard time overcoming the same thing. Because the test is now history for us, we judge harshly those who are struggling with the same. And so the very process through which God allowed us to undergo that we might be a means of comfort to others ends up being a tool of condemnation.

When we know of someone's pain we should pray to God to comfort the person in some way. That is always appropriate. We can never go wrong with praying. The question is, how will God answer? He may choose not to decree a miracle from His holy place. Perhaps He will not send angels to minister to the hurting. It could be that we are His answer to our own prayer. For the comfort we have received from Him is not to be kept to ourselves but given to others.

MEDITATIONAL THOUGHT: *Wounds have healing power*

Personal reflection: ______________________________

____

Prayer:

Dear God, You are the Lord of all my comfort. Help me to become a better steward of ministering to others out of the very comfort I receive from You. Teach me Your ways in this regard ....Amen.

12. Gifts Without Repentance

For the gifts and calling of God are without repentance (Romans 11:29)

God has provided each of us with those special abilities we need to bring to pass His purpose for us. We don't always measure up to His will. Thanks be to God that His calling upon our life and the gifts He has imparted to us do not vanish when we serve Him below par.

We must not view His gifts to us in isolation. They do not abide alone. Rather, they are imparted upon individuals who have been called to serve the body of Christ at large. Furthermore, no one has been born literally perfect, and God does not withhold the gift until we fully mature. Rather, we are growing while at the same time trying to fulfill our divine purpose. We are prone to error this way. When we do, God does not change His mind about the gift or the calling.

More than once, prominent servants of God have done things to bring reproach upon the gospel. Some of them lost the big ministries they led. Their misdeeds shook the faith of members of the family of God. Some who failed this way went off the scene for years. When they returned, what was often apparent was that the very gift for which they were once known and loved remained with them. Their failure did not surprise God. The gift did not flee with the reproach. God imparted the gift and calling upon them fully aware of what lay ahead.

Whatever gift God has given us for serving Him is forever settled in the heavens. He will not change His mind about it. No person or set of circumstances in life can alter that reality, though sometimes we may feel so far from God we can't even imagine that what He has bestowed upon us is still with us.

We are stewards of God's gift(s) to us. He wants us to glorify Him with the same. As He has faithfully entrusted us so let us faithfully utilize the gift, striving to be the best steward we can. Yea, let not the gift of God be imparted in vain but let us make it a great divine investment. One that will render great yield for the Kingdom, that in the end we will hear Him say, "Servant, well done."

MEDITATIONAL THOUGHT: *Divine investments—handle with care*

Personal reflection: ________________________________

____

Prayer:

Dear Lord, Thank You for not giving up on me when I fail to measure up to Your will in my life. Your calling upon my life and your gift(s) to me are forever settled. I will use them for your glory and not my own.... Amen.

13. Gathered in His Name

For where two or three are gathered together in my name, there am I in the midst of them (Matthew 18:20)

The power of the church gathered together lies neither in the prominence of the people nor in the value of their number. Neither the grandeur of her buildings nor her fiscal might defines her power. Rather, the power of the church gathered lies in the Lord's promise to be in her midst. Not perhaps He will be there, I say, but with certainty He will be present—one with His people, sanctioning in heaven their petitions and decrees on earth.

How should the power of this truth move us? What difference should it make to us knowing that the assembly of God's people invokes His presence? Not the assembly of dignitaries with streets and buildings named after them, mind you. Not the gathering of world leaders who are household names. Not even the convening of great physicians who give their lives to facilitate healing of the sick and wounded. But it is the gathering of the people of God united in the name of our Lord.

Most of us will never come in the official presence of an earthly king. Not because they are nonexistent. All civilized nations have a leader who could be deemed their king. Rather, because our person has been weighed and found wanting. Kings will never know our name. Not one of our requests will they regard.

But when we gather in the name of the Lord, the King of all kings shows up among us. Let us not dethrone Him of the occasion to be glorified by coming in His presence with doubt and divided minds. He wants to do great and mighty works among us. No challenge of ours is too great for Him. None of life's mountains are too high; none of its valleys too low.

Let us therefore hasten to the house of our God. Or let the saints convene at some other venue. Just let faith saturate the air. Sing praises to His matchless name. Let earth's agenda give way to that of heaven. And let the requests of His people be made known on high. Thusly, we are gathered in the name of our Lord. He is ready, willing and able to do great things among us.

MEDITATIONAL THOUGHT: *God never shows up empty-handed*

Personal reflection: ______________________________

____

Prayer:

Dear Lord, Thank You for the local assembly You have blessed me to belong to. I will not forsake the assembly of the saints. I will hasten to the house of God, yielded to Your will, expecting to see Your glory....Amen.

14. Healing the Brokenhearted

The Spirit of the Lord is upon me, because he has anointed me to preach the gospel to the poor; he has sent me to heal the brokenhearted... Luke 4:18

Twenty years ago, I was driving to Charleston, SC. Once I got there I couldn't find the place I was looking for. For the first hour after I arrived, I went around in circles, as lost as I could be. The traffic was terribly jammed. I could not recall other times during which I had seen traffic so bad.

Meanwhile, I happened to tune into a radio talk show. People were calling in, discussing their ordeals. I was not really paying attention. I just wanted some noise as the traffic and my being lost worked on my patience.

But when this particular man called in to the station, the hurt out of which he spoke grabbed my attention. I don't think I'll ever forget how hurt he sounded. He said his then-deceased dad was a drunk. While drinking, he did an evil routine: he ranted to his wife about how no-good their son—the caller—was.

The caller said the constant downgrading wounded him deeply. So much that, 25 years after the death of his father, the caller still bore the pain. Because of it, he said he hated his father. With much pain in his voice, the caller pleaded with parents listening: "Watch what you say."

Wounds so deep don't go away with time. They don't give you weekends off as some employers do. Neither can you call time-out as athletes can. Meanwhile, life goes on. So it is that many of the wounded go through life mustering a smile, trying to appear OK when they are far from that.

When God sent His Son Jesus, He had people in mind just like the caller I mentioned above. Because God sent Jesus to heal the brokenhearted, He is anointed for the task. That means God has specially equipped Him to heal those who have been crushed on the inside.

We are strong yet we are weak. A man, for instance, who stands as a giant in the business world, can be brought to a pitiful state by the loss of his precious little child. A woman, beautiful and vibrant, may abandon her desire to live after learning of her husband's infidelity. A champion of an athlete gets a terrible report from his physician, ending his bigger than life career. The good news is that God has sent and anointed Christ to heal the brokenhearted.

MEDITATIONAL THOUGHT: *Human physicians have limits*

Personal reflection: ______________________________

____

Prayer:

Dear Lord, You are the Healer of my heart and soul. When I am wounded, crushed from within, You are the healing balm that makes me whole from the inside out.... Amen.

15. The Light of Life

Your word is a lamp to my feet and a light for my path (Psalm 119:105, NIV)

It was St. Patrick's Day, 2008. The place was my hometown, Savannah, GA. It has one of the largest St. Patrick's Day celebrations in the country. Since the holiday that year fell within a holy week, the parade—during which time many revelers get really drunk—was moved to Friday, March 14. That Saturday night the celebration continued.

About 10:30 p.m. on Saturday night, the people were on our River Street partying. Suddenly, the electrical power went out in about two-thirds of the entire county. An estimated 150,000 to 170,000 people were out celebrating on River Street. Revelers panicked. They groped in the darkness looking for family members and friends and trying to find their own way. The only source of light was that which the policemen could provide from their flashlights and car headlights.

Even familiar settings can seem strange in total blackness.

The psalmist wrote the verse above during a time there was no exterior lighting as we currently know it. The darkness we experienced during the abovementioned St. Patrick's Day was the norm during biblical days. There was no such thing as your local power company to provide a source of lighting. Candles and lamps enabled the people to see where they were going and to foresee danger ahead such as a snake or criminal in their path. As these instruments of physical light were to people back then, so is the Word of God to us today. It gives us direction for life. It lets us know where danger is and tells us how to avoid it. When we study the Bible faithfully, it gives us light for life.

Go to your local bookstore, and you will find lots of how-to books on countless subjects. Many of the so-called experts have written books in their areas of specialty. Sometimes the writer is not considered an authority, but he has experienced personal success in some area of life such as losing weight or finding happiness. That becomes his credentials. Some of these books become bestsellers. The best counsel for our life, however, is the Word of God. In it we can find God's guidance on any area of life. More importantly, we will never go down the wrong path when we walk in the light of His infallible Word.

MEDITATIONAL THOUGHT: *The "blind" can't see the light*

Personal reflection: ______________________________

____

Prayer:

Dear Lord, Thank You for the light of Your Word. Unlike this world, I don't have to walk in darkness. As I study Your Word and You grace me with understanding, I will walk in the light and shun the darkness....Amen.

16. Hiding His Word

Thy word have I hid in mine heart, that I might not sin against thee (Psalm 119:11)

To significantly impact our life, God's Word must go deeper than into our ear. It must get into our heart. There, in accordance with the soil it finds, the Word takes root and with time comes to fruition. The resulting fruit will be after its own kind. Having come from God, the yielded fruit tends to the character of God.

We must guard the Word that has been planted into our heart. We should treasure it as a priceless find, for that it is. No price can we place on the value it will add to our life—if we allow it to come to fruition.

Interestingly, one of the main enemies to this process is life itself. Tragedy has its way of challenging our resolve. When we study the Bible and learn about God's faithfulness to hear and answer our prayers, and when we hear sermon after sermon on the same, these tend to embolden our faith in God. But during our hour of testing, it is possible that we will pray many times about our ordeal and see no evidence that God is answering us.

During such time, we may feel tempted to make light of the truths we received gladly into our heart before. This we must guard against so the Word that has become planted in our heart can do its intended work.

The value we place on an item can be known by how protective we are with that valuable. The money we have is normally safeguarded in a bank, not in our home where thieves and robbers may come and steal it, for example. Vital records of the family and of our investments and warranties, wills, etc. are stored in a secured place. Anything potentially damaging to our image is purged from every file, shredded, and discarded so it is permanently safe from discovery.

But none of these come close to the value of the Word of God. At least that should be the conviction of God's people. It gives hope to the hopeless. It's the best counsel of life that one can find, food that feeds our spirit, and the words of eternal life to those who are lost. How much more then should we guard it once it has been planted in our heart so it can give us the greatest yield in life?

MEDITATIONAL THOUGHT: *The treasure is measured by its chest*

Personal reflection: ______________________________

____

Prayer:

Dear Lord, Thank You for Your precious Word. May I never take it for granted or become nonchalant in hearing it. Daily I will receive it into my heart as a precious treasure to be hidden and guarded…Amen.

17. His Word Abides Forever

For all flesh is as grass, and all the glory of man as the flower of grass. The grass withereth, and the flower thereof falleth away: But the word of the Lord endureth forever…(1 Peter 1:24, 25a)

Everything in life is temporary. Glamorous women may employ all types of strategies, including medical procedures, to cling to their beauty. With time, however, it gives way to the aging process. A new housing subdivision with all new houses becomes an old neighborhood and looks dated with time. But God has given us the Word of God, and it abides forever.

Throughout the ages, there have been no updates to what God said in the beginning. This immutability is rooted in the fact that His Word is truth, and truth never changes. As an example, consider a simple law of gravity. It says that if you take an object that is heavier than air and release it, it will fall toward the ground because of the pull of gravity. No matter how sophisticated and highly technological our society becomes, such an object will never upon a free fall go upward into the air. It will always fall to the ground because this law is based on a truth, and truth never changes.

Similarly, the Word of God is truth. It has stood the test of time. Children sometimes say to their parents or grandparents, "You don't understand; things have changed since you were a child." Though that assertion is correct, still, the Word of God fits all generations to a tee. This is the Lord's doing, and it is marvelous in our eyes.

There are saints who have walked with God for over 50 years, living by His Word, and have found its counsel to always be faithful and true. The Bible has this unique quality because its Author is God. True, He used men to pen it all, but He was the Author. Holy men spoke and wrote as they were moved upon by the Holy Spirit. God used tens of writers at different times and places. Yet when the Bible was all assembled, perfect was the fit because the common thread that held it all together was that the Author was one. And what has that procured for us but the infinite wisdom of God's counsel that never fails?

MEDITATIONAL THOUGHT: *Truth is timeless*

Personal reflection: ______________________________

____

Prayer:

Dear God in heaven, Thank You for your eternal truths. They are an anchor for my soul in this crazy and ever-changing world. No matter what my circumstances are, I can always trust in Your Word....Amen.

18. Strength for My Weakness

And he said unto me, My grace is sufficient for thee: for my strength is made perfect in weakness…(2 Cor. 12:9)

We don't always feel strong, no matter who we are. We all experience times of weakness. This because life will certainly search out the limit of what we can bear, find it and test it. But that's the time we can experience God's strength the most.

He has given each of us strength in measure, enabling us to meet many of the challenges of life as if we are in control. We must not allow this strength to deceive us to think we are self-sufficient. To embrace this deception is to make ourselves prone to failing to acknowledge any need for or existence of help beyond ourselves.

Learning to trust in God's strength radically transforms our outlook on life. We become confident that no trial in life can overwhelm us. For what test is greater than God's strength?

There are many who have been tested in the past, certain they would not survive the severity of their trial. Even by the greatest stretch of their imagination, they could see no way out. Somehow times without number, these have found themselves on the pleasant end of the possible outcomes. The difference was God's strength that was perfected in their weakness.

This is a powerful truth. That is, that God is strongest in us when we are weakest in ourselves. Because of this we are much more resilient than we can imagine. Amazing it is how much suffering and adversities some believers can endure before God brings them out of their ordeal. As we observe them we might think to ourselves, "God you've gotta do something before this person is broken beyond repair." But that's not what happens. While the suffering continues with time, there is an inner strength that rises to the occasion. God has wrought this wonder in all of us.

The mystery of this strength cannot be experienced when all is well because it's not at work then. There is no way to do a trial run. We must trust God's faithfulness to be our strength in times of weakness.

MEDITATIONAL THOUGHT: *Human strength has been weighed and found wanting*

Personal reflection: ________________________________

____

Prayer:

Dear Lord, You are my strength when my own fails me. You have designed it that way. I will depend on Your strength in my times of weakness...Amen.

19. No More Than We Can Bear

God is faithful, who will not suffer you to be tempted above that ye are able...(1 Cor. 10:13)

Life isn't fair. It deals bad hands to all of us at one time or another. Some trials cannot be prevented even with the most proactive plans of prevention. The vehicles by which adversities arrive are too many to count or guard against. They may come through caring enough to help someone else, through errors in judgment when intents are good, attacks of our enemy the devil, our own misdeeds, etc.

Since God allows us to be tested at times, there must be some good in them, and there is. Trials offer opportunities for spiritual growth. They press us closer to God. They bring life to certain Scriptures as we are driven to apply them to the test. On the other hand, tests have the potential of being devastating.

Is not our Maker most qualified to be the steward of our tests? Omniscient, He knows our strengths and our weaknesses, and the magnitude of the difference from person to person. He customizes His stewardship accordingly so that no ordeal will break us beyond repair.

People tend to turn to desperate acts when they feel they are at their wits' end. Some turn to drugs, alcohol, or suicide as means of escapism, for example. Depression lurks at the door whenever hopelessness and despair exist. We the people of God should not be so moved. Our knowing and believing that He will not allow us to be tempted beyond what we can bear stabilizes the soul when things look gloomy. For we walk by faith and not by sight.

Nobody knows what the future holds for any of us. That's one of the reasons we obtain various kinds of insurance: automobile insurance because accidents can and do happen; homeowners insurance to protect our home and its contents; life insurance in the event of an untimely death; and health insurance so medical expenses won't wipe us out financially. But there is one vital kind of insurance that can't be procured on earth. Only God can insure that the trials of life will be kept within the boundaries of what we can bear.

MEDITATIONAL THOUGHT: *God is our best insurance*

Personal reflection: ______________________________

____

Prayer:

Dear Lord, Thank You that every test I am confronted with is subject to Your approval. If You allow me to endure the trial, it is because You know I can bear it. I will embrace this truth no matter how unbearable my load might seem…Amen.

20. The Message of Creation

The heavens declare the glory of God; and the firmament showeth his handiwork....There is no speech nor language, where their voice is not heard (Psalm 19:1, 3)

When we look up to the heavens, how glorious is the sight. We see the stars that rule by night and the sun ruling by the day. With each new day we behold the beauty of this earth, the divers kinds of trees, the beauty of many flowers, the roaring of the seas, and the majesty of the lofty mountains.

These communicate a very powerful message: there is a Master Architect of the universe. Surely this grandeur could not have resulted from a big bang, nor could it be the product of happenstance. More importantly, the message the creations communicate is universal.

Breaking the language barriers is one of the greatest challenges to world evangelism. To do this, the Bible must be translated into the various languages. The same has to be done for TV and radio broadcasts and inspirational literature, etc. But in all of the countries throughout the world God has planted witnesses for Himself. They never cease to proclaim Him. Before missionaries reach foreign soil, these witnesses are already there, endearing the true God to the natives. Namely, they are His creations.

Since the beginning of time, the earth continues to turn. The sun has never ceased to shine. Neither have the moon and the stars. They move about their divinely mapped courses with precision. Astronauts and scientists explore space, never ceasing to be amazed.

The more we learn about the creations, the more we stand in awe of the wisdom of God. They declare His handiwork. There is undoubtedly more to be known than there is that we know already. But we need not go to such depths. If we simply behold the wonders of the sun, the moon, the stars and clouds in the sky, and the flying creatures of the air, this will suffice. Their declarations are universal. No translators are needed. Whether you live in America or Africa, Poland or Pakistan, Brazil or the Bahamas, the witness of the firmament is clearly understood: only by the hand of an Omniscient and Wise Creator can this be so.

MEDITATIONAL THOUGHT: *The smallest creation is a great wonder*

Personal reflection: ______________________________

____

Prayer:

Dear Lord of the heavens, I marvel at the wondrous works of Your hands. They reflect Your glory. They testify of Your wisdom, setting You apart from all others that men refer to as gods. I worship You as the God of all creations....Amen.

21. Acknowledging God

Trust in the Lord with all thine heart; and lean not unto thine own understanding. In all thy ways acknowledge him, and he shall direct thy paths (Proverbs 3:5-6).

If we truly believe that God knows best, we should learn to acknowledge Him in all of our ways. That does not mean we make a decision on our own, and then go to Him to voice our intentions with no desire to hear from Him. If we expect Him to rubber-stamp our every whim, why should we go through the ritual of talking to Him about anything? Rather, to acknowledge God means that we pray to Him for guidance. We search the Scriptures to find out His will in the area of our concern. And we are willing to make course corrections to bring ourselves in line with His revealed will—before proceeding with our plans.

When we do this, the Bible says God will direct our paths. What's so special about that? He is omniscient. He perfectly understands all things. He sees all factors that bear on a matter, though many of them may be hidden from us. It is out of this superb perspective that He guides us. We can never go wrong acknowledging Him.

The Bible calls on us to acknowledge God in *all* our ways. That means this practice must become a way of life for us.

We all have witnessed the effects of bad decision-making. How often has a marriage started off as if it were perfect with two persons madly in love with each other only to end up hating each other? I submit to you that these couples did not get up one day saying, "I just feel like getting married and making a mess of my life." No, the truth is that life can be hard to figure out. Relationships are certainly hard to predict. That's why we need God to help us.

Our life is made up of many important decisions. Sometimes one wrong turn in life can cost us for the remainder of our existence. Hence, our quality of life is largely dependent on the decisions we make. God has many ways by which to direct our paths, though He speaks to us primarily through His Word. Let us desire to hear from Him daily. And when He speaks to us, let us walk in His counsel.

MEDITATIONAL THOUGHT: *Haste often makes waste*

Personal reflection: ______________________________

____

Prayer:

Dear Lord, I want to acknowledge You in all of my ways. I hereby renounce all tendencies to lean to my own understanding. Increase my sensitivity to perceive Your directions....Amen.

22. Higher Than the Heavens

Who is like unto the Lord our God, who dwelleth on high, Who humbleth himself to behold the things that are in heaven, and in the earth! (Psalm 113:5-6)

When we think about heaven, we imagine a perfect place. It is referred to as the throne of God. There, His glory abounds. His will is perfectly carried out by the heavenly hosts. But imagine this: God has to humble Himself to look on heaven! This revelation should take our concept of the holiness of God to another level.

That He must humble Himself to behold the things on earth we can understand. In our decrees and practices, we have declared all out war on Him in the name of the separation of church and state. And we have unleashed a blatant tide of immorality in the land. But He must humble Himself to behold the things in heaven as well. This is not to say that God looks on heaven with a condescending look. It is He who created the heavens and everything within them. He saw that everything was all good, meaning everything met His approval. But God's holiness sets Him above even the heavens.

We have no way of grasping what the psalmist is revealing. Sometimes places or experiences on earth leave us speechless. "You have to see it to believe it," we might say. But whatever we are talking about pales in comparison to what it would be like for us to visit heaven even for one minute. This I say on the authority of the few things the Bible reveals about heaven. Neither the English language nor any other is capable of adequately describing the celestial grandeur. Now consider that God has to humble Himself to behold such glory!

This picture of God is both humbling and emboldening. Humbling, because it is this God whom we strive to please. We can never completely measure up to His standards. All of us sin and fall short of His glory. Hence, we can be saved only through grace. Not one person on earth will boast in heaven that he earned his spot there.

Emboldening, because even though all of the above is true, we can have fellowship with this awesome God. He wants us to talk with Him. He desires to speak back to us. He has called us to be fellow laborers with Him to save the lost. He is genuinely concerned about our every struggle. If we trust Him, He will fight our every battle. Behold, what kind of love has the Father—higher than the heavens—bestowed upon His children!

By these two means, let us come into His presence: humbled by His greatness, emboldened by His love.

MEDITATIONAL THOUGHT: *To worship another as God is the greatest blasphemy.*

Personal reflection: ________________________________

____

Prayer:

Dear God in heaven, In prayer I enter Your awesome presence. No words can adequately describe the glory of that place. You must humble Yourself to behold heaven, yet You desire my time with You. There is no more glorious place on earth to be than in communion with You....Amen.

23. Divinely Protected

There shall no evil befall thee, neither shall any plague come nigh thy dwelling. For he shall give his angels charge over thee, to keep thee in all thy ways (Psalm 91:10-11)

Danger is all around us. Even if we don't go looking for trouble, it will seek and find us. So it was that on September 11, 2001, thousands of innocent people went to work at the Twin Towers as they normally do. Inside, it was business as usual. But outside was another story. Radical terrorists had commandeered commercial jets, turning them into weapons of mass destruction, killing and injuring thousands, and leaving a wound in America's soul that has yet to heal.

Granted, this was an extreme event. The point is that the victims were innocent people going about their noble routine of working to provide for their families and loved ones. And then it was terror like we have never known. How can we be safe in a world like our own?

No matter how careful we are, we can't be careful enough. Our local police force works hard to keep us safe, yet crime continues to rise. Everyday, innocent victims die or are injured at the hands of drunken or illegally drugged drivers. Who knows when a student on a high school or college campus or a customer at the mall or in a restaurant will go on a senseless shooting rampage?

We must trust God to protect us. He is our only dependable source. He can give His angels charge to keep us in all our ways. No matter where we go, they are there. When we pray we must believe this to be true, and God will honor our faith.

Both locally and nationally, trouble and danger make the news every day. We must not allow the media or even reality to dictate how we should feel. The message of this world might be perceived to say we must live in fear. But that's not what God says in His Word--not to those who walk with Him. We need not live in fear as those who know not the Lord.

We do not ignore the danger of our times. Neither should we be nonchalant, saying God will take care of us. But we must pray in faith for His protection, believing that beyond mortal view, there is an angelic host under divine orders to keep us safe.

MEDITATIONAL THOUGHT: *God is our refuge*

Personal reflection: ______________________________

____

Prayer:

Dear Lord, You are my peace amid this troubled world. Thank You for Your divine protection. Help me to not embrace the fears of this world....Amen.

24. His Kingdom Come

Of the increase of his government and peace there shall be no end, upon the throne of David, and upon his kingdom.... (Isaiah 9:7a)

Jesus taught His disciples to pray "thy kingdom come." He referred to the Kingdom in several ways during His teachings. He said, for instance, the Kingdom of God is within us. He also taught a number of parables, saying "the kingdom of God is like...." In these, He gave us Kingdom principles we ought to live by while on earth. But ultimately Christ will establish a literal Kingdom here. It won't be just another kingdom as the kingdoms of men. No reasonable comparison will exist between the two.

While here on earth, we the people of God are in this world, but it is not our home. We are sojourners in this place. The decrees of men often rival the commandments of our God, causing conflicts in our soul. We long for a Kingdom where righteousness rules. This will not be realized until the Lord reigns on earth. On the throne of David shall He sit. Then shall the will of the Lord be perfectly done on earth as it is in heaven.

When His Kingdom comes, two things will never end: increase and peace. How can there be no end to increase? Can it go to infinity? This is an idea mortal minds cannot visit. But with great joy we receive this truth because the Bible says it will be so.

As for peace, it has escaped us through the ages. So many lives have been lost fighting for the same. Yet the world today is in as much chaos as it has ever been. The people of the nations, by and large, look to their government to resolve the serious tensions between hostile nations. All kinds of peace treaties have been signed and truces have been made—with little success. When all else has failed, the Prince of Peace shall come and war will be no more.

So many problems currently plague our land. The answers from the kingdoms of men will no longer suffice. The time of their effectiveness is racing to a close. Solutions by and large have escaped this earth. All the world's greatest men together will not be able to solve the crises. The world may lament the times, but we can rejoice because our redemption draws nigh. The Kingdom of our Lord is at hand.

MEDITATIONAL THOUGHT: *Our end is eternity with no ills*

Personal reflection: ______________________________

____

Prayer:

Dear God, I am in this world but not of it. You are the King of my soul. I want You to reign in every area of my life....Amen.

25. A Merry Heart

A merry heart doeth good like a medicine: but a broken spirit drieth the bones (Proverbs 17:22)

Observe those who have a positive attitude toward life. Even when times are trying, they can keep a smile and remain cheerful. Seldom can you tell that they are going through a bad experience because they don't let that alter their countenance. There is a benefit at work within them that is not apparent to the naked eye. Having a merry heart is more than just having a merry heart. This disposition does a person good like a medicine.

What empowers one to live the life of the merry-hearted? It is a hope-filled life. Hope in God, that is. Hopelessness, on the other hand, causes the spirit to be broken, opening the door to depression, which in turn can be debilitating.

God's will for us is that we live our lives trusting Him. The better we learn to do that, the more merry-hearted we will be. We will live our lives filled with hope and expectancy, knowing that whatever we face in life, it pales in comparison to the awesome God who's on our side. The ultimate goal is for us to get to the point that we believe nothing is hopeless, and that God is always working on our behalf. This kind of attitude about life will positively affect us on many levels. Plus, it will infect those around us.

A merry heart is not happenstance. It is not an automatic disposition assumed when we become Christians. It is a matter of choice. Yes, there are those who attend church week after week to hear the good news preached, say Amen to the many promises of God as the preacher preaches, study their Bible often, and who pray to God as well. Yet they stay down in their spirit. It is when these spiritual activities are mixed with genuine faith in God that a person can have a positive attitude about negative experiences.

Being a Christian does not mean we don't experience tough times on earth. On the contrary, we go through many of the same things unbelievers do. But we need not despair because we have God on our side. Having Him on our side makes all the difference in the world. This truth is the source of a merry heart, and it will do you good like a medicine.

MEDITATIONAL THOUGHT: *Physician, heal thyself*

Personal reflection: ________________________________

____

Prayer:

Dear Lord, You are the strength of my heart. When trouble comes, I know You are very present. Help me to remain positive about life. I want my joy and inner peace to infect those around me....Amen.

26. New Mercies

It is of the Lord's mercies that we are not consumed, because his compassions fail not. They are new every morning: great is thy faithfulness (Lam. 3:22-23)

When Adam sinned against God, the penalty fell upon us all, making us sinners destined for death eternal. This fate was determined for us before we left our mother's womb, and before we had done anything either good or bad. Some have cried foul. Why, they say, is it our fault that Adam sinned? We would not have done what he did had we been him, they add.

Eventually, God sent His Son to redeem us from the curse of Adam's misdeed. After making this provision, God could have left us on our own to determine our eternity. How bad would that have been for us? Though through the blood of Christ we have been made new creations, we cannot walk flawlessly before God from that day forward 'til death. Every new creation in Christ has proven that.

As babes in Christ, not knowing what to do, we did what we knew. As we grew in Christ we learned what to do, but not being fully mature, we didn't know the best way to do what we did. At spiritual maturity, we were yet fallible so though we knew what to do and how to do what we knew, we often missed the mark. Between each success and each failure God's mercy was there for us. No matter how often we placed a demand on His mercies, they were always there. They never ran out because they stemmed from His inexhaustible compassions for us, and they were new every day.

There have been many great servants whom God has used mightily. For many of them, books have been written of their achievements. Those are the things we remember most about them. But equal to or excelling their deeds are God's many mercies they experienced along the way. These are often not mentioned in the book. If they are not, then the complete story has not been told. Every great woman and every great man in Christ has known God's mercies times without number.

Our journey to greatness or to maturity is not without opposition. We have an adversary the devil, and he has but one mission. It is to devour the people of God. The war the enemy wages against us is what makes life a press. There is but one reason we will win the struggle. It is because the Lord's compassions they fail not. They are new every morning: great is His faithfulness.

MEDITATIONAL THOUGHT: *God doesn't give us what we deserve*

Personal reflection: ______________________________

____

Prayer:

Our Father, I often thank You for the things You have brought me through, the things You bless me with, and for the things You enable me to accomplish. But this time I want to thank You for the many times You've shown me Your mercies instead of Your judgment.... Amen.

27. All Things Through Christ

I can do all things through Christ which strengtheneth me (Phil. 4:13)

A young minister came to a troubled congregation as its new pastor. This was his foray in pastoring. He was scared and excited at the same time. Scared because there were lots of unknowns about what the job entailed. Excited, because he dreamed of conquering the world for Christ.

In less than three months he met his first crisis. He sought the many resources he had received from his seminary training. Nothing he found in them was a good fit for the challenge at hand. He turned to the advice of respected and more seasoned spiritual leaders. Their counsel he found to be priceless. The ministry was one test after another.

After ten years had passed, the congregation held an appreciation celebration for this pastor. At the close of the meeting he was asked to make a few remarks. He stood and reflected. Two things he learned, he said. One, he had to forsake his own way and to meet every challenge with much prayer, faith, patience, and the rich counsel of the Scriptures. Two, through these helps he had come through every past test, and through them he was confident he could meet any challenge that lay ahead. "I can through Christ," he boasted.

The young minister exemplified one of the main differences between a new convert and a mature Christian. It is the degree to which each utilizes Christ in his life. Babes in Christ tend to do what they have always done. Oftentimes, not knowing what to do, they do what they know. The mature, on the other hand, has learned to operate more effectively through Christ.

The key word above is *learned*. As we grow and experience Christ we learn that He is the source of our greatest strength. The more intimate this lesson becomes to us, the stronger we become. Not because it enables us to shoulder more but because we learn to maximize our resources in Christ.

We can't even begin to fathom the depth or measure the breadth of what we have in Him. Greater dimensions are revealed as we walk with and experience Him. No test in life can come close to exhausting our strength in Christ. The mark of our maturity is that this truth has become our testimony.

MEDITATIONAL THOUGHT: *Christ is more than enough*

Personal reflection: ______________________________

____

Prayer:

Dear Jesus, I covet maturity in You. Teach me how to make You the total strength of my life. Speak to my heart regarding those areas in which I have not fully learned to appropriate the resources I have in You....Amen.

28. Hope in God

I had fainted, unless I had believed to see the goodness of the Lord in the land of the living (Psalm 27:13)

Observe a person being tested in life, and who has no hope of a better day. The resulting despair becomes the engine that drives his life—more appropriately called death. For it is not life when one cries for the day at night, and longs for the night at day. It is not life to abandon all occasions to laugh or even smile. It is not life to cease all conversations with God.

It's not the presence of the test that ushers in this death but the absence of hope. As the people of God we should always expect to see His goodness pervade our darkness. We should not find this to be a great leap of faith. He has promised to never forsake us, and He cannot lie.

One of the most treasured benefits of studying the Scriptures is that they give us hope in God. And why hope in God? Because our hope can be no better than the object of our hope. And hope makes not ashamed when God is our hope. He makes all things work together for our good.

This hope is not wishful thinking. It is not dreaming. It is not kin to denial of reality. But hope is a positive expectation based on our trust in God. Its presence means despair is not. It gives us vision to a way forward. Songs of praise precede the manifestation of our expected end. Through hope the energies of the soul are kindled.

Such hope we build through the Word of God and prayer. Our experiences with God over time also promote this hope. Furthermore, we need the encouragement of others who walk with the Lord. For hope comes also through corporate edification.

We should build strong hope before the evil day comes. Just as wise men of war prepare for battle in the time of peace. This analogy is not without significance. Our enemy the devil has declared all out war against us. In our own strength we are no match for him. But not one of his assaults can permanently move us when our hope is founded in God. Moreover, the end of this hope is always His glory.

MEDITATIONAL THOUGHT: *God is the author and rewarder of our hope in Him*

Personal reflection: ______________________________

____

Prayer:

Our Father, Precious is my hope in You. I am tested in many ways just as those who don't know You. The difference is that I trust in You. When I am greatly tested, my desire is to showcase my hope in You .... Amen.

29. Beholding His Glory

Then said I, Woe is me! for I am undone; because I am a man of unclean lips, and I dwell in the midst of a people of unclean lips: for mine eyes have seen the King, the Lord of hosts (Isa. 6:5)

When men of the Bible sensed they were in the presence of God, their reaction was not one of joy but of fear. Those close encounters stemmed from a special relationship they had with God. Still some regarded the visitation as a death sentence. It was the holiness of God against the wretchedness of men that occasioned such dread. To them a serious "protocol" had been breached. How could mortal men be found in the same room with His majesty?

There is no darkness in Him. His purity is off the scale. He must humble Himself to look on heaven, and that is His throne. Even the darkness is like light to Him. The intents of our heart are naked before Him. The more we learn about Him, as revealed in the Scriptures, the more we stand in awe of Him.

He called Moses upon a mountain, and commanded him to build the tabernacle. He showed him the pattern after which to make the tent. This was done to the intent that God could visit His people. When we gather in His name, we should expect more than a religious gathering. What separates the assembly of believers from other convocations is that God visits His people.

But where has He gone? Some ask this question because the glory that the people of God in the Bible experienced seems rare today. The answer is that God and His church have grown far apart. He is not the one who has moved but we are. To experience His glory, we must mend the breach.

God's glory does not reside in the common place. It's in a secret place of the Most High. Only those whose heart pants after Him can find this place.

Our relationship with God is based on faith. Though we can't see Him, we know He is ever present. When we pray in faith and walk with Him, we know He hears and answers our prayers. But when we experience His glory—whereby He manifests His presence in some awesome way—this is His way of saying to us, "this is a special moment between us."

MEDITATIONAL THOUGHT: *The glory of God is not happenstance*

Personal reflection: ______________________________

____

Prayer:

Dear God in heaven, I cherish my time with You. Teach me how to tarry in Your presence. And help me to forsake those things in my life that deny me that special place in You….Amen.

30. A Higher Source

...when my heart is overwhelmed: lead me to the rock that is higher than I (Psalm 61:2)

During the 2008 presidential election, much criticism was leveled against the war in Iraq. The justification for why we were even there was questioned. The hundreds of billions of dollars that had been spent to fund the war was another issue. And then there was the death toll of our young soldiers and the tens of thousands of those who had been permanently wounded.

Another cost raised its ugly head as well. It was the rising number of suicides and the emotionally traumatized among our soldiers in Iraq.

They had been trained to fight and defend their country. Nevertheless, what they were being subjected to was way too much—even for men and women of our military. The human soul is not designed to endure such prolonged ordeal.

If men and women of war have limits beyond which they become overwhelmed, how much more so is this true for the rest of us? We all have limits. God has made us that way. He is our higher source. To Him we must go when a test takes us out of our league.

A key to successful Christian living is for us to learn how to give God the things we are not designed to handle. Too often we fail in life because we neglect doing that. When we pray for God to give us the strength to do these things ourselves, we do so amiss. He does not equip us to do what He has reserved for Himself.

Several church members who served in different capacities in their local church found themselves getting on each other's turf. One person thought it was her responsibility to perform a certain task while another thought it was his. The confusion came because they had not been trained by church leaders as to what their roles were. They did what was right in their own eyes, and it just wasn't working. Sometimes, something that needed to get done did not because everyone thought it was somebody else's responsibility. Proper training to know what each person's roles were quickly solved this problem.

Similarly, we have two types of challenges in life. Some of them, God has equipped us to handle. The others, He has reserved for us to look to Him. A vital key to success in life is for us to discern between the two, and to act accordingly.

MEDITATIONAL THOUGHT: *God's load is too heavy for us*

Personal reflection: ______________________________

____

Prayer:

Father, I thank You that I can come to You whenever life is too much for me alone. Not one of my problems is any match for You. Teach me how to give You all the burdens that overwhelm my soul....Amen.

31. Grace to the Humble

God opposes the proud but gives grace to the humble" (1 Peter 5:5, NIV)

Grace is unmerited favor from God. By it, we are saved when we believe on Christ's redemptive work on the cross. Without God's grace, none of us can be saved. By our own works we can never measure up. Moreover, God's grace causes the clouds of the seemingly impossible to give way to bright sunshine. By grace, the tests God suffers to touch the lives of others don't come near us. The list goes on and on. For God's grace manifests itself in infinite ways.

To abound in His grace, we must walk humbly before Him. This statement is not without significance. Humility is not incidental to our becoming a Christian. When our spirit became born again, our flesh, by and large, remained the same. Ask the pastor of any local church. It is simply not true that all he has to do on Sunday mornings is to convey the will of God to the people of God, and then consider it done. On the contrary, disobedience to God is commonplace in a local church.

Happy are we when we abound in God's grace. It is sufficient for us, no matter what our challenges are in life. Sometimes, God chooses to not answer our prayer the way we ask Him to, though there is nothing amiss about what we are asking. Neither does He have a bone to pick with us. In those instances, He gives us sufficient grace for the matter at hand.

We are assured that one of two things is always true when we walk humbly before God. One, He grants us our requests in prayer; or two, He grants us the needed grace. Why should we care if when we pray to Him to remove a heavy burden, He chooses instead to give us the wherewithal to endure the same? Either way, the objective is met.

The grace of God is indispensable in the life of a Christian. How often we miss the mark of God. But He does not zap us every time we fail. When we walk humbly before Him, He shows us His kindness, even amid our failures. Thank God for His amazing grace.

MEDITATIONAL THOUGHT: *Attitude often determines altitude*

Personal reflection: ______________________________

____

Prayer:

Our heavenly Father, I so desire to walk humbly before You and to abound in Your grace. Help me in those areas in my life in which I struggle to submit to Your will….Amen.

32. Servants are Great

...whoever wants to become great among you must be your servant (Matthew 20:26, NIV)

It was January 18, 2009, over 40 years since his death. Tens of thousands lined the streets during the annual parade and festivities to reflect on his legacy. People from diverse ethnic and religious backgrounds united for the cause. What made this man, Dr. Martin Luther King, Jr., so great in the eyes of so many Americans? It was not because of his oratory skills, though exceptional they were. He was a man of great courage and faith in God. He confronted a racially divided America, steeped in social injustice, and challenged her to embrace her creed.

But that's not what made him great. Simply put, he was one of the greatest Americans in history because he served humanity. And so his life speaks on.

Jesus taught that we attain greatness in the Kingdom by being servants. This runs counter to the way the world thinks. It teaches us that the great are those whom others serve. The more subordinates they have the greater we esteem them to be.

Jesus also modeled greatness in the Kingdom. He was God incarnate. Being our Creator, He could have flexed the muscles of His Lordship. Nevertheless, He came on earth to serve and not to be served. By this spirit, He obeyed the cross and death. As His disciples, we must follow His lead. For if He was God and He served us, how much more so should we serve each other?

The greatest mark of discipleship is not the keeping of the Ten Commandments, or maintaining perfect church attendance, or belonging to a number of ministries in the church, etc. Rather, it is to serve others. Busyness in the local church is often used interchangeably with servanthood, since the purpose of the church and the ministries therein is to serve. This is not necessarily the case, however, since our labor can be heartless.

Now that Christ has returned to the Father, He wants to live His life through us. There is but one indication that this is occurring. It is that we have submitted to serving others. Then as Christ was in the world so are we. The church has no force on earth more powerful than her love in action. As has been often said, the world does not care how much we know until it knows how much we care.

MEDITATIONAL THOUGHT: *We serve God by serving others*

Personal reflection: ______________________________

____

Prayer:

Dear Lord, thank You for Your Son Jesus who died on the cross for my sins. I want to follow Him more completely. Help me to serve You by serving others with the heart of a servant....Amen.

33. Our Place of Treasure

...Lay up for yourselves treasures in heaven....For where your treasure is, there will your heart be also (Matthew 6:20-21)

A man flew his company's plane almost a thousand miles to take a five day class to further his professional development. About an hour into the first day, he received a call on his mobile phone. Hurriedly, he left the class. Throughout the morning, he repeatedly left the room. At lunch, he shared with me what the problem was. His broker had called him to tell him of the losses that were occurring in the stock market. The two tried frantically to minimize the man's losses. He had already lost tens of thousands of dollars that first morning of class. He said he couldn't concentrate on what was being taught. His heart was on his money.

In this man's actions, we see a powerful truth. Wherever we store a treasure, our heart becomes focused thereon. This can be seen in a mother who is overly protective of her child. All through the day, no matter where she is physically, her heart will be with that child. She may be out on a special evening with her husband and having the time of her life, but she will call, or at least be tempted, to check on the apple of her eye.

Jesus taught us to lay up treasure for ourselves in heaven. Thereby He calls us to make the Kingdom of heaven our priority while here on earth. The resources and time we commit to the Kingdom must exceed those we devote to our earthly endeavors. No other mindset will please the Lord.

When an avid investor awakes and finds that the stock market has crashed, he is greatly moved by the terrible news. His neighbor, who has not one penny invested, awakes to the same news, and switches the TV channel to something else. Having laid no treasure there, his heart is not on Wall Street.

Similarly, our failure to lay up treasure in heaven breeds indifference. Having nothing invested, we feel no sense of ownership. Passively waiting for a change of heart is not the cure for this spiritual apathy. Rather, one must be proactive and lay up a genuine treasure in heaven, and afterward his heart will go there too. Many places exist on earth that we can lay up a treasure for ourselves. But only a treasure in heaven pays throughout eternity.

MEDITATIONAL THOUGHT: *Heaven is our best investment*

Personal reflection: ______________________________

____

Prayer:

Our heavenly Father, I thank You for the privilege to invest in the Kingdom of heaven. So many other things in this world vie for my attention. But I will keep my heart focused on heaven....Amen.

34. The Power That Works in Us

Now unto him that is able to do exceeding abundantly above all that we ask or think, according to the power that worketh in us (Ephesians 3:20)

We can't gauge the power available to us through Christ. What He provides us is off the scale. The fullness of this awesome power, however, is not what we actually experience. The only portion that becomes personal is the amount that effectively operates in us.

Neither our words nor our thoughts can go where God's ability can. No human concept of His power comes even close. He can do far beyond what we ask or think.

Since God's power available to us is off the scale, whatever problem we have is but a light thing for Him. But that fact is not enough. We must know how to appropriate this power so it becomes our reality. For instance, it's a fact that we have enough food in America to feed all of its citizens. But we still have many Americans who lack ample food each day. Our adequacy of food is no consolation to those who don't experience the benefits. Similarly, no matter how capable God is, no matter how astounding the lyrics are in the songs we sing about His greatness, and no matter how many confessions we give about the same, the only thing we can personally relate to is the degree to which we experience this awesome power of God in our lives.

Oftentimes, we are guilty of regarding God as if He were a man. Greatly tested, for instance, because we can't see a way out, we tend to feel there is none. Such hopelessness can send you into depression, if you let it. But God's ability to deliver us is not subject to our ability to understand how He can. Our thinking is limited, but His power is not.

To experience more of God's power in our lives, we must die to ourselves. The more we can do that, the more we can live for Christ. He does not force Himself on us. He takes control of the portion of our lives we willingly give Him. His will, of course, is for us to totally die to ourselves so Christ can live through us completely. Thereby we bridge the gap between the power available to us and what becomes our personal experience.

MEDITATIONAL THOUGHT: *Realization of one's potential is not born of chance*

Personal reflection: ______________________________

____

Prayer:

Dear God in heaven. I want to experience more of Your power in my life. Help me to die to myself more completely so Christ can live in me more abundantly....Amen.

35. Childlike Faith

...Except ye be converted, and become as little children, ye shall not enter into the kingdom of heaven (Matthew 18:3)

If we want a picture of the kind of relationship we must have in the Lord, we need only to watch a little child and his trust in his parents. He thinks no guile toward them. He trusts their words, even when they defy logic. Knowing he can do nothing without them, he depends on them for everything. He feels safe in their arms.

The irony is that children are born with this simple and pure trust in their parents, but Christians must grow up to become as little children in their faith in God. That is, it is only by spiritual growth that we can arrive at the point of trusting God's promises, even when they don't make much sense to us. There is no shortcut to this place. Christians who have childlike faith in Christ are those who have worked at it over time.

The process by which we arrive at this type of trust in God resembles that by which two friends do. Trust between them doesn't just happen. One must be willing to make himself vulnerable to the other in some way. Trust can never grow between two people who keep their guards up all the time. When we trust someone, however small at first, it affords the other person the chance to prove himself to be trustworthy, and so the trust factor grows.

Many times, Christians read the promises of God that speak directly to their situation. They will even say they believe that if they obey Him in that area, they will see a turnaround. But the stickler is that the promise requires them to make themselves vulnerable that God might prove Himself trustworthy, and they often find that difficult to do. Alas, some Christians go through their entire pilgrimage never learning how to become as children in their faith in God.

A noteworthy contrast exists between God's people in biblical times and those of today. During the former, before the explosion of knowledge we currently know, men seemed to have childlike faith, and God used them greatly. Moses obeyed the Lord, stretching forth the rod in his hand to open the Red Sea that the nation of Israel might pass over. At Jesus' invitation, Peter walked on water.

Nowadays, with all the knowledge about the Bible we have gained, we have complicated the subject of faith. Slews of books have been written on what is faith, and how to have it. This itself is a true sign that we have strayed from childlike faith. There is no mystery or difficulty. Faith simply obeys God.

MEDITATIONAL THOUGHT: *Knowledge puffs up, but God has chosen the poor to be rich in faith*

Personal reflection: ________________________________

____

Prayer:

Dear Lord, I want to have childlike faith in You. I want to move beyond the intimidation of my circumstances. I don't want to be wishy-washy toward Your promises. I ask You to help me in my areas of unbelief....Amen.

36. A Quiet Voice

And after the earthquake a fire; but the Lord was not in the fire: and after the fire a still small voice (1 Kings 19:12)

Oftentimes, in the Bible when God manifested His presence, He did it in a dramatic way. He caused, for instance, the rain to fall 40 days and nights when He judged the world in Noah's day. To destroy Sodom and Gomorrah, He sent fire and brimstone on earth. When He called Moses to lead Israel out of Egypt, fire appeared amid a bush that was not consumed. He sent an angel on earth to announce the birth of Christ our Savior.

These dramatic occurrences should not become our theology on how God speaks to us or how He manifests His presence. Oftentimes, however, in gatherings where worshipers display ecstatic behavior, many take that to mean God is in the place. Conversely, they regard quiet gatherings as "dead" and void of His presence. But God shows up in quietness, also. There, He speaks to us in a still, small voice.

We live in a terribly loud world. Airplanes take off and land all the day. Noise pollution from cars plagues our large cities. Most Americans have at least one mobile phone, and use it they surely do. Just how did we survive without those little wonders in the past? Our youths glue themselves to video games and social networking web sites, and they drive their cars with music so loud it's almost deafening.

God does not shout above this clutter. To walk with Him, we must slow down the pace and turn down the volume of life, thereby enabling us to hear His voice. As we study the Bible and pray and meditate, He speaks to us today just as He spoke to His people in days of old. But it is in the quietness of the moment that His quiet voice speaks loudly.

How often has God spoken to us, and we heard not a word? We looked for a sign from heaven, but there was none. No angelic visitation. No voice that shook the earth. No one who met us with a prophetic word, and told us what only God could have revealed. "Why do I cry to You, and You answer me not?" we cry. And so we resort to the more dramatic, if haply that would get His attention. But still no answer. Perhaps there was an answer from Him. Not in a visible sign but in a quiet voice. Let us learn to hear Him there.

MEDITATIONAL THOUGHT: *The Lord's voice is seldom audible*

Personal reflection: ______________________________

____

Prayer:

Dear Lord, life is full of decision-making. I need you to order my steps. Give me wisdom, and give me ears to hear Your quiet voice when You speak to me....Amen.

37. Wonderfully Made

I will praise thee; for I am fearfully and wonderfully made.... (Psalm 139:14)

Out of all of God's creations, there is but one He made in His image and in His likeness. Since He is a Spirit, the reference to our being in His likeness and image has nothing to do with our physical qualities, God having none of these. The core of our being is spiritual, and it has been fashioned after God. That we have been made in His image is a mystery too deep to fathom. At a minimum, it means we have been wonderfully made. We are the only creation He has made for having fellowship with. For none of His other creations did He send His Son all the way from heaven to die for and to redeem.

Though many significant scientific breakthroughs have occurred over time, we have only scratched the surface in understanding God's prized creation. Consider, for example, the human brain. It weighs on average about three pounds. It contains about 50-100 billion neurons, of which about 10 billion of them pass signals to each other via nearly 10 trillion synaptic connections, experts say. The most advanced computer today pales in comparison to the sophistication of the human brain.

There are those who argue that we resulted from evolution. That is, over time we evolved from lower forms of life that predated us. Others say we are the product of a big bang. From this disorder, say they, came forth the universe. But God says we are the work of His hands. He cannot lie. That settles the debate for people of faith. Behold the brain spoken of above. Who else but our awesome God could have created such wonder?

Each of us on earth is unique. That is, we are not carbon copies of others, but we are divinely designed originals. This is true of every one of the more than seven billion people on earth. Yet we often make the mistake of trying to be like someone else, and that is all we can do—try. No one can beat us at being the person God made us to be.

Before the foundation of the world, He decreed a purpose for each of us. We must make it our mission to find and embrace that purpose. If we fail to do so, we will leave a void in the earth that no one else can fill.

MEDITATIONAL THOUGHT: *God made all originals and no copies*

Personal reflection: ________________________________

____

Prayer:

Dear God in heaven, thank You for making me so special. No one else in the world is just like me. Help me to fully embrace the wonderfully unique person You have created me to be....Amen.

38. Thanks in Everything

In every thing give thanks: for this is the will of God in Christ Jesus concerning you (1 Thessalonians 5:18)

It was dark and raining as I drove west on the interstate. Suddenly, I saw a pair of headlights coming toward me. The car of the person some distance in front of me was hydroplaning. His car had spun 180 degrees, and was now moving east in the westbound lane. I had never experienced this before. I'd read about some of the do's and don'ts of what to do whenever it occurred. One thing I remembered was that you should never ride the brakes. So I took my foot off the accelerator, tried to avoid the car that was coming toward me in a rather wobbly fashion, and hoped for the best. One thing working in my favor was that I saw no cars in my rear view mirror, as far as the eyes could see. That gave me liberty to turn however I needed to, to miss the approaching car, which I successfully did.

Needless to say, I thanked God for how things turned out. But what if it had not ended that way? What if, instead, my car did collide with the oncoming car, and I was injured to the point of hospitalization? In the latter case, giving God thanks would have been more difficult. But we must be able to render to Him thanksgiving in all things. Note, thanksgiving *in* all things, not *for* all things.

Most of us can find much room to be more thankful to God. One area involves those routine things He does for us such as waking us up each morning, blessing us with a job to go to each workday, and enabling us to pay our monthly bills. He does these things for us so faithfully for so long that we take them for granted. Then there are those painful situations we find ourselves in and that can even make us feel bitterness toward God. Our personal feelings must have no part in this matter. Because the Bible says that in everything we must give thanks to God, He has already determined that He is thankworthy at all times.

Our attitude toward thanksgiving reveals where our heart is with the Lord. For the immature and the unbeliever, thanksgiving tends to be subjective or conditional. The mature believer has learned that true thanksgiving is not based upon our circumstances or feelings but upon the person of our God.

MEDITATIONAL THOUGHT: *God is never the enemy*

Personal reflection: ______________________________

____

Prayer:

Dear Lord, forgive me for taking Your goodness for granted at times. Regardless of my circumstances, You are thankworthy. Teach me how to make thanksgiving a way of life....Amen.

39. Healing for Our Land

If my people, which are called by my name, shall humble themselves, and pray, and seek my face, and turn from their wicked ways; then will I hear from heaven, and will forgive their sin, and will heal their land (2 Chronicles 7:14)

If we objectively view the vital signs of our nation, we will conclude that it is gravely ill. Crime plagues most of our large cities. In some places, drought conditions have placed our resources for adequate drinking water at dangerously low levels. Our national debt currently exceeds 17 trillion dollars! Corruption seems to be commonplace in our government at the local, state, and federal levels.

What will be our end, if we allow the current course to continue? Hopefully, we will never know, but we will declare war to stem the tide. Reality, however, poses some serious questions to our quest. How can we solve our crime problem? No legislation or size of police force can succeed. What can we do about our growing water shortage? God has exclusive rights to the waters from on high. And how can we substantially reduce the national debt? We have shown over the past decade as this monster has been consuming us that we are not willing to make the serious lifestyle and fiscal changes needed.

The bottom line is that we have a mess. Our nation is critically ill, and needs to be healed. Only God can do that, and only His people can move His hand in that direction. Everyone can pray to God, Christians and unbelievers. But the only ones He has obligated Himself to hearing and responding to are those who believe on His Son Jesus and who also walk humbly before Him.

God blesses the nation whose God is the Lord. This declaration is not a call to make America a Christian nation. We are far past that as a possibility. Christianity is simply one of many religions tolerated in our country. Notwithstanding, a strong correlation exists between the blessings of a nation, and how much that nation allows God to be her Lord.

The leaders of our world have a different take. They would have us to believe they don't need God. They insist that a rigid line be drawn between religion and government. This decree is tacit self- confidence that they have all solutions and control their own destiny. But look at our current plight. If ever there was a time we've needed God to intervene in the affairs of our nation, it is now. We must become broken before Him for our land. Through an engaged body of Christians, He can send revival in the church. He in turn can change the hearts of men in high places. He can radically change the spiritual climate of our land. In short, if we humble ourselves and fervently seek His face, He can heal our sick land.

MEDITATIONAL THOUGHT: *God is not an option but our only hope*

Personal reflection: ________________________________

____

Prayer:

Dear Lord, I stand in the gap for our nation. We desperately need Your intervention. Increase my burden for our land, for the lost, and for our leaders….Amen.

40. Taste and See, The Lord is Good

O taste and see that the Lord is good....(Psalm 34:8)

How often do we take time to think about and meditate on the Lord's goodness to us? This He shows us times without number. Since we went to bed last night, He has kept us safe from danger. This is not without significance. Many who slept last night did not fare as well. We may be so bold as to think that it was because of the precautions we took and because of how special we are to God. The truth is that He kept us.

He also blessed us to awaken this morning, and to see another day. Being over 55 years old myself, He has done this for me over 20,000 times! It becomes increasingly easy to begin taking this goodness of the Lord for granted. To be sure, there was someone who was younger than we are and healthier than we who did not awaken to the land of the living today. Each morning we get up on this side of the grave, we should savor the Lord's goodness in this regard.

How did we end up where we have in life, wherever that is? To me, this is one of the greatest mysteries in life. Or should I say, it is one of the greatest testaments to God's goodness to us. The answer to this question is bigger than the magnitude of our personal efforts, though it has its place. For instance, most of you reading this book were not born in a third world company, but you could have been. The fact that we were not has nothing to do with the choices we have made. For where we were born predated any actions taken or choices made on our part. Simply, the Lord has been good to us.

When we taste and see that He is good, not only does this please Him, but also it becomes food for our soul. That's because how we feel about ourselves impacts how we view life. A child's spirit went to the dumps because she lost in a contest she wanted to win badly. Mom took her in her arms, and pumped her up by reminding her of all the wonderful things she has going for herself. The champion in her came alive again, and she looked beyond the minor defeat.

The enemy would have us to believe that God has forsaken us, especially when we are being tested, and it looks as if God is nowhere to be found. In such times, we can minister to ourselves by thinking on and recounting the Lord's goodness. Even in the worst of times, we won't have to look far to find plenty evidence of His goodness in our lives.

MEDITATIONAL THOUGHT: *Even bad times are seasoned with God's goodness*

Personal reflection: ______________________________

____

Prayer:

Dear Lord, thank You for Your goodness You show me daily. Please forgive me for my complacency. I will stand still and savor Your goodness more often....Amen.

41. Prayer and Temptation

Watch and pray, that ye enter not into temptation: the spirit indeed is willing, but the flesh is weak (Matthew 26:41)

Christians never stop being human. We will always have desires in our flesh with which we must contend. With time, we learn to walk more in the spirit and less in our flesh. But the flesh will always present challenges for us in this life.

Denying ourselves of the very things we like is difficult. But that is what we often have to do if we want to please the Lord. In the Scriptures, Paul the apostle refers to his flesh as a body of death. We are clothed with this enemy of our spirit until death does us part. That's why we must pray to God daily for help in denying our flesh and obeying our spirit.

Our flesh is one of the most powerful weapons the enemy has against us. He tempts us with those things that appeal to our humanity. These include greed, sexual gratification, power, and money. Many of the ills of our society have their roots in one or more of these. That mere fact is a testament to the power of influence these temptations wield over the flesh.

Men have been falling prey to the weaknesses of the flesh since the first man and woman God placed on earth. Why should the devil change his strategy? The exploitation of our flesh has proven to be effective throughout the existence of humanity. Great men have been brought to infamy through the weakness of their flesh. Some who are currently destined for greatness will never come near their full potential for the same reason.

We dare not leave this area of our Christian walk to chance. Neither should we ignore the areas of our flesh in which we struggle. Those who do so will meet certain defeat. We must actively pray for God to help us. When we do, He gives His angels charge to keep us. He imparts to us whatever we need to win the war against our flesh.

Some weaknesses of the flesh are stubborn. They may appear to be unbeatable. Sometimes it seems as if the more we pray, the more pronounced our fleshly struggles become. But we walk by faith and not by sight. If we continue to pray in faith, God will cause us to prevail in every area of our life. No struggle of our flesh is as great as His power.

MEDITATIONAL THOUGHT: *The more we bow to God, the less we bow to flesh*

Personal reflection: ______________________________

____

Prayer:

Dear Lord, thank You for changing me on the inside through faith in Christ. You have placed a new spirit in me that pants after Your heart. As I strive to walk in the Spirit, strengthen me in those areas in which I struggle in my flesh....Amen.

42. PRIESTS TO GOD

But you are a chosen people, a royal priesthood, a holy nation, a people belonging to God, that you may declare the praises of him who called you out of darkness into his wonderful light (1 Peter 2:9, NIV)

Every Christian today is a priest to God. Accordingly, we can enter His presence and offer sacrifices. This privilege was not extended to the congregation at large during Old Testament days. Instead, the priests from the tribe of Levi went to the Lord on the people's behalf.

As New Testament priests, what shall we offer to God? The Old Testament priests offered the blood and flesh of animals. These offerings were a foreshadow of the perfect offering that was yet to come, Jesus Christ the righteous. Now that He has come and offered His life for our sins, we have no need to offer animals and their blood. He has made atonement for us once and for all.

As priests today, we offer those things that abound to God's glory. For instance, the Bible commands us to offer ourselves as a living sacrifice. That means we must be a living offering to God. This seems like a dichotomy, since a sacrifice denotes something that is put to death. But this is how a Christian is supposed to live—alive to Christ and dead to self at the same time. Blessed is the priest who masters this sacrifice. All of his ways will please the Lord. Whatever he does shall prosper.

As priests, we also offer the sacrifice of praises by exalting the name of our God with the lips of our mouth. God in turn inhabits our praises. That's why sometimes when we pray to God, we should refrain from asking for anything. Instead, only bless the name of our God. He in turn will inhabit our praises. In the Old Testament, as the priests were doing service to God, sometimes the glory of the Lord filled the place. It was so overwhelming that the priests could not continue their service. This was a sign that their offerings pleased the Lord.

In the Old Testament, the priesthood was limited to the tribe of the Levites. Only they were ordained to do the service of the sanctuary. In effect, the rest of the congregation was at the mercy of the priests. In the New Testament, the priesthood has been expanded to all who are in Christ. We don't need anyone else to go to the Lord for us. We can enter His presence at will, and bring to Him our sacrifices.

MEDITATIONAL THOUGHT: *God deserves the best we have to offer*

Personal reflection: ________________________________

____

Prayer:

Dear Lord, thank You for the privilege to enter Your presence. Thank You for Jesus our High Priest who made it all possible. I will live my life as an offering acceptable to You ....Amen.

43. Our Intercessor

...the Spirit itself maketh intercession for us with groanings which cannot be uttered (Romans 8:26b)

One of the greatest testimonies regarding the value of prayer—or more accurately, the indispensability of prayer—in the life of Christians is the fact that the Holy Spirit makes intercession for us. When we experience difficulty, so severe that we don't know exactly what to pray for or how to pray correctly, the Holy Spirit does so on our behalf. Belonging to the Godhead, the Spirit always prays according to God's perfect will. That He has given us such an Intercessor to help us is proof that our prayers alone have their limits. And in times of great testing, we need effective prayer.

Every Christian needs dependable prayer partners. But these can be hard to find. If you believe statistics and polls, most believers spend only a few minutes a day in prayer. It is reasonable to assume that most of that limited time is devoted to praying for themselves and not for others. And at times, have we not all promised to pray for someone else and failed to do so? Or at least we were not as zealous as we should have been. But the Holy Spirit is our trustworthy prayer partner. His intercession is not audible. Nor is it in lieu of our own.

When we are tested, God allows us to be stretched in our own prayer life. These are opportunities for us to grow. On the other hand, He knows when tests become so overwhelming that we don't know how to prevail through prayer. He knows where that place is for each of us. Accordingly, the Holy Spirit intercedes on our behalf so that when we press our way in prayer, not one but two of us are gathered together in the name of the Lord.

That God has provided us deity to pray for us should dispel the notion that what we pray for and how we pray is not important. This is not overkill. It attests to the seriousness at hand. There are those who believe that simply going through the religious motion is all that's required. Moving God through prayer, however, requires more than a ritual. Prayer can be warfare. It must be in accordance with truth, it must be passionate, and it must be under girded by faith. Our Intercessor from heaven always prays this way for us. Thanks be to God for His unspeakable gift.

MEDITATIONAL THOUGHT: *The Holy Spirit prays perfectly—always*

Personal reflection: ______________________________

____

Prayer:

Dear Lord, thank You for the Holy Spirit who intercedes for me. He helps my infirmities in the area of prayer. With His help, I can embrace each challenge in my life with faith and boldness.... Amen.

44. His Truth Endures Forever

Thy word is true from the beginning: and every one of thy righteous judgments endures forever (Psalm 119:160)

Many things have changed since the time God dealt with patriarchs such as Abraham, Isaac, and Jacob. We no longer travel primarily by foot and beast, but by automobiles and mass transit. No one reading the Scriptures in Moses' day could have imagined a day such as ours in terms of the knowledge explosion we are now experiencing—except God Himself.

The truths He gave His servants who penned the Scriptures are just as trustworthy today as they were when He first gave them. Their time limit is the end of this age. Nothing throughout the generations will require any addenda or revisions thereto.

This means we can trust the Bible to work for us today and tomorrow. Though things in our world change so fast we can hardly keep up, the Word of God is timeless. Through it, parents of all generations can teach their children the perfect way in which they should go when they grow up. God is the Author of the Bible, and truth is its pillar.

The value of the Word of God is not that it gives us another strategy for life. Rather, it is the only trustworthy guide for life. At the fall of man in Eden, our compass was rendered defective. We ended up so far from the truth, we had no idea of how to find our way back. The worst thing we can do now is to lean upon our own understanding, and many have done precisely that. This is evident in the way the world of unbelievers persecutes those who remind it of the error of its ways. Biblical truths that define our moral values, once the norm, are now branded as extreme. Those who choose to do what's right in their own eyes have proven times without number that doing so leads to the wrong place every time.

We don't know what tomorrow will bring. Some of our modern day doomsday prophets predict "the perfect storm" is in the making. Most of us at the least will admit that a lot about tomorrow remains a big question mark. Regardless to what our future holds, however, the Word of God will be just as trustworthy then as it was when God spoke it through His servants, ages ago. When we walk in these truths, they become an anchor for our soul. Success and victory will always be our end.

MEDITATIONAL THOUGHT: *Truth is not subjective*

Personal reflection: ______________________________

____

Prayer:

Dear God in heaven, I praise You for the timeless truths of Your Word. I will not be moved by the uncertainty of this world. I will trust in Your Word....Amen.

45. Greater is He in Us

...greater is he that is in you, than he that is in the world (1 John 4:4)

It's ominous, and the signs are everywhere. You can see the evidence on the local, national, and international news. It is the way of this world, defying all reason: hackers determined to invade secure networks, aimed at shutting down their own government's operations; terrorists bent on bringing disaster to the nation's airline industry; gruesome killings of infants and teens; a woman stealing another woman's unborn child by cutting it from her womb; teens sexting; corruption at the highest levels of government, etc.

The culprit is the devil himself. He rules the spirit of this world. He writes the script that this world must follow. All who know not the Lord God are subject to the spirit of this world. Like a playwright with a deranged mind, the enemy takes the script to places our minds can't go. There is no predicting what the next act will entail. Nor is there any earthly weapon that can defeat his evil works.

Those of us who know Christ are not subject to the spirit of this world. We have been translated from the kingdom of darkness to the Kingdom of light. A greater One now lives on the inside of us. His Spirit abides with us forever.

It is not enough, however, for Christ to live on the inside of us and for us to be delivered from the spirit of this world. Equally important, we must live a life of being led by the Spirit of Christ who indwells us. Since Christ and the devil diametrically oppose each other, evidence that we are being led by His Spirit is reflected in the fact that we don't walk according to the way of this world.

Unbelievers should see the stark contrast between us and themselves when they look on us. Some, no doubt, will want the liberty wherein we walk, and wonder why they can't just follow suit. This very dynamic makes us the light of this dark world. Through this lifestyle, we endear the Holy Spirit to the lost, generating questions about our liberty, and creating opportunities for our witness and the work of the Holy Spirit. These are the possibilities when the greater One not only lives but also works on the inside of us.

MEDITATIONAL THOUGHT: *No one can be free when his spirit is bound*

Personal reflection: ________________________________

____

Prayer:

Dear Lord, thank You for delivering me from the spirit of this world. I don't have to walk as unbelievers do. Help me to live my life each day so others can see the awesome liberty I enjoy in Christ who lives in me....Amen.

46. He Abides Faithful

If we believe not, yet he abideth faithful: he cannot deny himself (2 Timothy 2:13)

The Bible says we walk by faith and not by sight. That means our life should be driven by the promises of God and the principles of His Word. But sometimes it's hard to walk by faith because of what we see with our eyes or because of human nature.

Take the prophet Elijah, for example. When Israel tried to serve God and the idol Baal, Elijah challenged the people at Mt. Carmel to choose whom they would serve (see 1 Kings 18). After God proved Himself to be the true God by sending down fire, Elijah ordered the false prophets to be put to death. Elijah showed himself to be a man of faith in the Lord on that day.

But when the news came to Jezebel, the wicked wife of the wicked king of Israel, she sent word to Elijah. She warned that within 24 hours she would have him killed. You would think that after what God had just done at Mt. Carmel, Elijah would have met Jezebel's threat with a bold response. But that's not what happened. Elijah ran for his life, and requested to God to die.

All of us can relate to Elijah in some way. Sometimes we do great in walking by faith. At other times, however, we do terribly. I have learned through observations that many, if not most, Christians have one area or more where they really struggle to trust God. But in the other areas of their life, walking by faith is not a problem.

Consider a church pastor who is faithful in discharging his ecclesiastical duties as a shepherd. He believes in the authority of the

Scriptures, and preaches from them each week with passion. Church members thank God often for having sent them a Bible-believing shepherd. On the other hand, there is one thing he constantly wrestles with. It is his desperation to see God change his ministry situation. He preaches to his congregants about God's faithfulness to provide for their every need. Yet, he is often tormented by the financial condition of the ministry. He can hardly rest at night if Sunday's monetary offerings are low.

Our flesh and the devil our enemy will use our personal struggles against us because we know we are failing God in that area in which we struggle to walk by faith—whatever that area is. We must bear in mind that we are not to put our trust in our own faith but in Christ's faithfulness. When our heart is right toward God, even in areas in which we fail to believe as we should, Christ remains faithful to us.

MEDITATIONAL THOUGHT: *Faithfulness is unconditional*

Personal reflection: ______________________________

____

Prayer:

Dear God in heaven. Please forgive me for my failure to walk in faith at times. In my heart I strive to trust You in all areas of my life. But my faith is not in my ability to measure up to Your standards. My faith will rest in the ever-abiding faithfulness of Your Son....Amen.

47. Hope Through the Scriptures

For whatsoever things were written aforetime were written for our learning, that we through patience and comfort of the Scriptures might have hope (Romans 15:4)

When God inspired men to pen the Scriptures, He had us in mind. One of the main ways He speaks to us today is through the records of His dealings with His people during biblical days. The objective is that through these accounts we might have hope.

The Scriptures provide for us the preponderance of evidence that God is faithful. Not one time do we find in the Bible where a person truly trusted God and the Lord failed him. Though these accounts date back thousands of years, because the Lord never changes, they still apply. If we also walk in a similar trust in God, He will not fail us as well. It behooves us then to study the lives of men and women in the Bible who walked with God and who enjoyed His blessings, that we might enjoy a goodly lot.

Moreover, the Scriptures testify of God. They reveal His ways, which cannot be discovered by human adventure. The more we study the Bible, the bigger and more awesome our God becomes. The challenges before us will pale in comparison thereto.

Also, as we study the Scriptures, we edify ourselves. We live not by bread alone, but by every word that proceeds from the mouth of God. In turn, our fears give way to boldness, faith, and hope.

The Bible is a priceless heavenly treasure. Nothing on earth can compare to it. Let us open and draw from the riches of the Scriptures every day. In doing so, we feed our faith—or starve our doubts. Everyone who does so will love life. Not because things will always go well for those who place their trust in God. Trials belong to the just as well as the unjust. But it's because the Scriptures assure us of a pleasant end when we place our hope in God. All who forsake this heavenly treasure will be destitute of the hope, since it can come only through our trusting God.

The Bible is a love message from God to us. Not only does He say times without number He loves us, but also He shows it. Not in abstract ways that require us to fill in the blanks, but through records of the experiences of people just like us who trusted Him and in the end experienced His faithfulness. Plus, God gave us His beloved Son who gave Himself for us. This collection of His love in action is our hope.

MEDITATIONAL THOUGHT: *Our hope is out of this world*

Personal reflection: ______________________________

____

Prayer:

Dear Lord, thank You for the Word of God. When I am tested, I can turn to the Scriptures for comfort. They are the source of my hope in life...Amen.

48. All Things for Our Good

And we know that all things work together for good to them that love God, to them who are the called according to his purpose (Romans 8:28)

God is in total control of everything. Some may question that, given the current course of this world. The news is filled with doom and gloom. So many heinous crimes occur today that some people ask the question, if there is a God out there, how can He allow the atrocities we see? Are His hands tied? Do we live in a deistic world, etc.?

God's in total control, but He does not micromanage the affairs of this earth. He gives us the freedom to make choices and to suffer the consequences thereof. One of the errors we make in assessing God's presence in this earth is that we tend to look for the evidence in the world at large. Conversely, what we see in the Bible is not so much God working in the world at large but in the lives of His people. We should not expect to see overwhelming evidence of His glory in this world because, by and large, it has rejected Him.

For those who love God, however, we should expect to see His hand at work in our life. He has an ultimate plan for us. This He decided before the foundation of the world. He will let nothing derail it. Sometimes things get so twisted in life and so cloudy that it's hard to see what road we are on. But God knows exactly where we are, and what end He has appointed for each challenge we encounter. All of His acts fall under the umbrella of His ultimate plan for our life and what redounds to our good for the present.

A teenage couple was viewing a movie they had rented. It turned out to be a real cliffhanger. The girl was on edge as the mystery unfolded and added to her emotional high. She looked at her boyfriend who did not seem to be fazed by the suspense. "You guys have no feelings," she commented. He in turn responded, "No, it's not that. I have already seen this movie before. I already know how it's going to end."

Sometimes, episodes in our life can be like cliffhangers. We need not fear the outcome, however, no matter how ominous things might appear. God has already promised that He will make them all work together for our good. He is always in total control.

MEDITATIONAL THOUGHT: *Our drive for today is fueled by our outlook on tomorrow*

Personal reflection: ______________________________

____

Prayer:

God, I thank You for managing the affairs of my life. You are the perfect steward. You always know what's best for me. During those times when I can't make sense of my life, I will trust You for a good outcome....Amen.

49. Not by Bread Alone

...Man does not live on bread alone, but on every word that comes from the mouth of God (Matthew 4:4, NIV)

We tend to think about food for our bodies all through the day. Many Americans actually think on food too much, as witnessed by our epidemic of the overweight and the obese. Food is important because we cannot function properly without the various nutrients we get from what we eat. The same is true on the spiritual side. But how often do we think about the Word of God as food?

Regularly studying the Scriptures requires a commitment of time. And most people are not just looking for something to do to utilize their time. They already have more to do than they have time for. The only way they will succeed in getting a regular diet of the Word of God is by making a commitment to do so. The time they devote to feasting on the Word of God must be deemed sacred.

The Bible contains everything we need to be spiritually healthy and vibrant. Regardless of the area of our walk with God that needs attention, the Bible is the best resource. The tendency of some, however, is to pick over the menu. Some people, for instance, only want to hear what the Bible says about healing, or material blessings, or spiritual gifts, etc. They search what the Bible says about these areas as one looks for a needle in a hay stack. They virtually ignore the rest of the Scriptures. Some of these people even search out a local church where the biblical teachings they prefer are the predominate teachings there. The problem with this mindset is that it cannot yield healthy Christians. If we want to be spiritually strong, we must make the entire Bible a vital part of our spiritual diet.

The Bible is not just another book; it is the Word of God. This is what separates it from all other literary works on earth. When we study the Bible and give heed to it, God is speaking to us. If we could literally take a trip to heaven, stand before the throne of God, and ask His counsel on any matter, not one time would He say anything to us that would conflict with the Scriptures! God and His Word always—always agree.

Reading the Bible helps to keep us built up in our most holy faith. Even when times are difficult, we can be bold and strong, if we are eating the awesome spiritual food that has come down from heaven to us. If we neglect to do so, we will end up a spiritual weakling.

MEDITATIONAL THOUGHT: *We are what we eat*

Personal reflection: ________________________________

____

Prayer:

Dear Lord, thank You for Your written Word. It is food for my soul and my spirit. I will maintain a love for Your Word so that I remain spiritually strong and healthy....Amen.

50. Ministers for the Saints

Are they not all ministering spirits, sent forth to minister for them who shall be heirs of salvation? (Hebrews 1:14)

When we think about angels, we tend to think of them in a lofty fashion. They stand in the presence of God, carry out His divine mandates, and travel from heaven to earth with much ease. They are empowered to do the miraculous, etc.

Ironically, one of the jobs of these special beings is to minister to Christians. From what we can tell from the Scriptures, God has at least millions of angels. If we could see what's happening in the spiritual realm, we would see that heaven and earth are buzzing with angelic activity. God made none of His creations only for the sake of making them. He never involves Himself with vanity. Because He created so many angels, and because they have a divine mandate to serve the people of God, we can conclude that He planned on much interaction between the angels and His people.

At times in the Bible, people saw angels. These events were few and far between. We should not take this to be the limit of angelic activity in the Bible. The truth is that angels are ministering spirits. As such, they are invisible—except for the times they manifest themselves. They were busily at work throughout biblical times. The same is true about them in this current day.

How special we must be in the eyes of God. He created us in His own image, created food for us to eat, and gave us dominion over everything He made on earth. If that wasn't enough, He created an army of spiritual beings whose charge it is to minister to us.

Though the angels have been sent to minister to us, they take not one commandment from us. God is the one who gives the angels charge. They do nothing except He bids them to. When we pray in faith and walk in obedience before Him, He orders the angels to minister to us as we need to be ministered to. It is He who has wrought within them the passion and the wherewithal to bring His will to pass.

In the quietness of the early morn, gaze into the morning air. Savor the peace and the absence of noise pollution before the streets are tainted with cars and people. By faith, moreover, fail not to see the following, though hidden from mortal view: There is an angelic host out there, diligently working on your behalf.

MEDITATIONAL THOUGHT: *Those for us are more and mightier than those against us.*

Personal reflection: ______________________________

____

Prayer:

Dear Lord, You are the keeper of my soul. You give Your angels charge to keep me in all my ways. I will not fear what life may bring ....Amen.

51. Praying with Confidence

And this is the confidence that we have in him, that, if we ask any thing according to his will, he heareth us (1 John 5:14)

When we pray, we may wonder if anyone in heaven is listening on the other end. One reason we may feel this way is because it can be a long time before God grants our request. Plus, most of the time, He gives no sign to assure us that an answer is forthcoming. The problem with our not being sure that God has heard us is that we can't have confidence about what to expect. This in turn makes it hard for us to have a bold confession. Instead, we may downplay our expectations, and take a "wait and see" attitude, which totally displeases the Lord.

It is imperative for us to know that when we pray, God hears us. To have this confidence, we must pray according to His will. It is to this end that God has provided us the Bible. It is the only source by which we can learn His ways, which in turn guides us on how to pray according to His will.

God always honors prayers that are offered up in accordance with His will. How confusing it would be for us if that were not the case. But He is never the author of confusion. He is always consistent so we can always be confident that when we pray according to His will, He hears us.

What do we mean when we say God hears us? Surely, He is not deaf. The truth is that He hears the prayers of every one. This should not be a hard thing to believe, since He knows even our every thought. But when we talk about Him hearing us, we are talking about Him actively hearing us, as opposed to some passive response to our prayers.

If we know God has heard us, we should be confident about receiving the answer to our prayers. His ability to deliver is never in question. If He can create the heavens, the earth, the seas, and all that is in them, what request can we make that would slightly challenge Him? Moreover, it is His pleasure to give us the Kingdom. He sent His beloved Son to die for us while we were yet sinners; now that we are the children of God, why would He not through the same Son freely give us all things? Prayer worked for Jesus and the apostles during their day. And God is no respecter of persons.

MEDITATIONAL THOUGHT: *If with confidence we pray, inner peace will follow*

Personal reflection: ________________________________

____

Prayer:

Thank You, Lord, for hearing my prayer. I am confident that I will see the fulfillment of my request. I will walk by faith and not by sight....Amen.

52. Inseparable

I am persuaded, that neither death, nor life, nor angels, nor principalities, nor powers, nor things present, nor things to come… shall be able to separate us from the love of God (Romans 8:38-39)

We can't begin to fathom the depth of God's love for us. The Scriptures are filled with statements of the same, but they don't do the subject justice. Even when skillfully used by the most prolific of writers, the English language—or any other—can't come close to describing God's love for us.

Let it suffice for us to know that no opposition on earth, in heaven, or in between can separate us from God's love. This is one of the most stabilizing truths in the Bible. Moreover, this love is unconditional. That is, not only is it true that He loves us this way when we strive to dot the I's and cross the T's, but also when we fail miserably.

Amid moral failures or failure to measure up to some standard of performance, we can be tempted to think of God in human terms. After committing what we regard as a horrible sin, for instance, instead of talking to Him about it, we may think we are the last person He wants to talk to or hear from. The truth is, that would make us one of the first persons He wants to hear from. He has no pleasure in our pain. Perhaps we are tempted to associate every bad thing that happens to us as God getting back at us. But He didn't fall in love with us because of our stellar performance in the beginning. Accordingly, our moral failures don't cause Him to fall out of love with us.

We should not view God's love as a weakness. He is holy. Our refusal or failure to walk humbly before Him will impact our relationship with

Him, in terms of how much He can use us to serve Him, and how intimate our mutual relationship with Him can be at the time. But His love for us won't allow Him to settle for that. He labors untiringly to bring us to the place where we belong. No matter how far we stray from Him and how strong the separation appears to be, we can always return to His loving arms, assured of no rejection.

God is not a man. How we feel about ourselves has nothing to do with how He feels about us. His love can't be understood by the human mind and, hence, the condemnations borne of men are to no avail. Nothing—absolutely nothing—on earth, in heaven, or in between can separate us from His love.

MEDITATIONAL THOUGHT: *God mended the breach with His own blood*

Personal reflection: ______________________________

____

Prayer:

Dear God in heaven, I thank You because no matter what I am going through, You are there with me. You love me with a perfect love. Help me to "wear" Your love for me each day that others might see it....Amen.

53. Yea and Amen are His Promises

For all the promises of God in him are yea, and in him Amen, unto the glory of God by us (2 Corinthians 1:20)

The Bible is filled with the promises of God. He used many holy men to scribe the promises, but these writers all "spoke" with one voice. The down trodden find reasons to hope and dream again through the good news of the gospel. Darkness may be all around them and as far down the road as the eye can see. But as to whether the light can shine again, the promises of God say, yea and Amen.

Things are so uncertain in this world. The anchors and foundations of our past appear to be failing on every hand. So-called experts have all kinds of theories on how to solve the pressing problems of our world. "If we take these steps, this is what will happen," they pontificate. A consistent testament of their track record is that things seldom turn out as they predict. This devilish truth is a main fuel that drives the political engine of our country. New candidates can always cite the performance record of the incumbents as reasons they are running, and boast that they can do a better job. But oftentimes, it's déjà vu all over again, as new politicians are dogged by their inability to solve the same old challenges. In this hour, we must place our hope in God and His promises. They will never disappoint us.

No matter how good promises sound to us and how uplifting we find them to be, they are no better than the person who makes them. In our case, the Maker of them is God himself. First of all, He cannot lie. Secondly, we count Him able to do according to all He has promised.

It behooves us to saturate our lives with His Word, so that we might be filled with His promises. When we resolve that we can't achieve a lofty goal, or overcome a difficult challenge, the Word of God never joins in on our pity party. It challenges us to believe in the awesome God of the Bible. Its mission is to translate us from doubt and nonchalance, to a bold faith in Him. The promises of God are contagious, if we stay in contact with them long enough. In due time they will infect our spirit so that it says to us in the midst of difficulty and the nay sayers, yea and Amen.

MEDITATIONAL THOUGHT: *God's promises are found in Christ*

Personal reflection: ______________________________

____

Prayer:

Dear Lord, thank You for the many promises found in Your Word. I know that every one of them has been ordained by You. If I place my faith in them, I will not be ashamed. I will boldly walk in this conviction….Amen.

54. Freedom from Slavery

For we know that our old self was crucified with him so that the body of sin might be done away with, that we should no longer be slaves to sin (Romans 6:6, NIV)

When we accept Christ, we become born again, freed from slavery to sin. Such a statement suggests that prior to this encounter, we were slaves to sin, and that is exactly right. This is not to suggest that Christians are sinless after meeting Christ. That is certainly not true. A world of difference exists between being literally sinless and being free from bondage to sin. Christians belong to the latter group, not the former.

Though we regard America as a free country, most of her citizens are slaves. Not at the hands of a human master, but of their own corrupt, innate nature. In this regard, all of us were born spiritual slaves, no matter where on earth our birth occurred. No decree from the highest court in the land can loose us from this bondage. That's why God sent His Son Jesus Christ to save us from our sin. Save us, I say, because but for Christ's intervention, our eternal damnation would be certain.

Just because we have been freed from the bondage of sin doesn't mean we can't or don't sin anymore. We are not literally sin free, neither are we immune to sin thereafter. We have been freed from sin's stronghold. We have been empowered to walk in the liberty that only Christ can give. If we are to realize victorious living, we must be fueled by this truth whenever we encounter moral struggles. Our being tempted to sin is not a sin; it is only when we submit thereto. The good news is that when we have Christ living on the inside of us, we don't have to allow sin to reign in our bodies.

The message of this world is that "everybody's doing it." Excess and sexual gratification seem to be the order of the day. Christ's will is that we not walk according to the way of this world. We must glorify Him in our mortal bodies. We must be living epistles of the liberty available in Him. Thereby the world can look on us and see that it is not true that everybody's doing it. This is not some psychological game. Christ radically changed us when we met Him. As He was crucified on the cross, so has our old nature been crucified. This was done to the intent "that we should no longer be slaves to sin."

MEDITATIONAL THOUGHT: *True freedom comes only through Christ*

Personal reflection: ________________________________

____

Prayer:

Dear Lord, I thank You for freeing me from spiritual slavery. From this day forward, with Your help, I will not allow sin to reign in any area of my life....Amen.

55. Guarding His Word

Thy word have I hid in mine heart, that I might not sin against thee (Psalm 119:11)

Jesus tells the story of a man who went about sowing seeds, some of which fell by the wayside. When His disciples asked Him about the meaning of the parable, He explained that when some people hear the gospel, the devil comes and steals the Word that was sown in their heart. The enemy still attempts to use this tactic against us. That's why we must with all diligence guard the Word that is sown in our heart.

Life itself can aid and abet the cause of the enemy. We can become so caught up in the busyness of life that we fail to exercise due diligence in studying and applying the Scriptures as needed to add depth to our convictions. If this neglect becomes pronounced, the Word we have heard will become distant—though it is near us, even in our heart. Like a precious seed that has been planted and needs to be cultivated, the Word must so be guarded. If we fail to do this, it will not yield its eternal fruit in our life.

If we want to please God, we must seek to know His Word. It is the only means we have for understanding how to please Him. A challenge to this end is the fact that His Word and our natural being are often diametrically opposed to each other. What might seem OK to us can in fact be abominable to the Lord. Our only chance of success, in pleasing Him, is to receive His Word as a precious jewel, guard it from all the enemies of our soul, and walk faithfully before Him.

Our world has declared all-out war on the Word of God. Not by verbal decree, but by the self-destructive course that it has chosen. Let us not be deceived, however. The devil himself, the prince of this world, is the one in the driver's seat. Those who don't know the Lord are subject to the spirit of darkness. What we see then is not what we have. We wrestle not with flesh and blood, but with the powers and rulers of the darkness of this world.

Meanwhile, we know that God is not the author of confusion. Not one time does He act against His Word. The two always speak with one voice. Hence, we are assured that whenever we obey the Word of God, we will not sin against Him.

MEDITATIONAL THOUGHT: *Neglected seeds yield substandard fruits*

Personal reflection: ______________________________

____

Prayer:

Dear Lord, Your Word is more precious than silver or gold. Nothing can compare to its rewards. I will be more diligent in safeguarding Your Word that is sown in my heart....Amen.

56. Divine Counsel

Thy testimonies also are my delight and my counselors (Psalm 119:24)

They say a picture is worth a thousand words. What is the worth of the accounts of God's works that have been recorded in the Bible? They testify of Him. They are written for our edification. God speaks to us through these divine records.

All of us have our so-called favorite Bible stories, such as Jonah and the big fish, Noah's Ark, Israel's crossing of the Red Sea, Samson and Delilah, etc. Parents teach these powerful stories to their children. Many also learn of them in Sunday school and children's church. But these were not placed in the Bible simply for our reading enjoyment. The question one should ask herself is what is God saying to me through this account? And what must I do to incorporate this counsel into my life?

Some Christians regard the Old Testament as irrelevant for today, mainly because we live in the New Testament era. But God never changes. His truths endure to all generations. He destroyed the world during Noah's day because of man's evil. We must take heed. Through this ancient account, He speaks to us today and to the generations to come: the same climate will usher in the same judgment upon this current world. It behooves us, then, to heed all the testimonies of God, from Genesis to Revelation.

Our need for God's counsel can be seen in our world today. Our challenges are progressively more daunting. There is poverty, war, budget deficits, homelessness, crime and murder, unemployment, etc. How did we arrive at our current dilemma but through leaning upon our own understanding? We know it was not God's doing. He is not the author of such confusion. But for generations we have made light of His counsel. Under the doctrine of separation of church and state, our government has all but banned Jehovah from inputting into its affairs. In our zeal to make the statement that we don't need God's counsel, we have shown in no uncertain terms that our wisdom alone is no match for the task.

When we delight in and hear the testimonies of God, we will discover a priceless treasure. They are more than doctrinal truths that we endlessly debate the meaning of. They show forth the nature and power of God. Through them, He speaks to us; yea, they are our counselors.

MEDITATIONAL THOUGHT: *God's testimonies are more than testimonies*

Personal reflection: ______________________________

____

Prayer:

Dear Lord, I thank You for the abundance of Your testimonies as found in the Scriptures. Give me ears to hear the depth of what You are saying to me through what You reveal by way of Your acts....Amen.

57. JEHOVAH-SHAMMAH (THE LORD IS THERE)

...and the name of the city from that day shall be, The Lord is there (Ezekiel 48:35)

A gathering in the name of the Lord is of little value without His presence. The former does not guarantee the latter. During Judah's captivity, God showed Ezekiel a vision. It had to do with the city and the sanctuary that would be rebuilt, the original ones having been destroyed by the Babylonians.

In the vision, God addressed the measurement of the city and the temple, the gates thereto, the worship that would occur within the temple, etc. Last of all, He said the city's name would be called "The Lord is there." This was the most important statement of all. The people had been led captive because they had strayed far from God. In effect, He was telling them that if they would forsake their transgressions and return to Him, He would be in the midst of His people.

In many ways, Judah in Ezekiel's day is a microcosm of Christendom today. I believe that many if not most of us would agree that the church today has strayed far from God. All is not lost, however. In the vision to Ezekiel, we have God's prescription for the healing of our relationship with Him. If we walk accordingly, the name of the church shall be called "The Lord is there."

Judah was in captivity, Jerusalem had been destroyed, and God promised to return them to their homeland and rebuild the city and the temple. But the vision He gave Ezekiel was ultimately for a much more distant future. Hence, in the midst of Judah's total disappointment to

God, He showcased His desire to dwell among His people. This is a testament to His undying love for them, in spite of their failures. Surely, we have all seen this unconditional love of God operating in our lives.

The Bible commends only one kind of relationship with God. It is one in which He is very present in the time of trouble. One in which He never leaves nor forsakes us. One in which He hears our every petition. Such a relationship with God is not happenstance. If it were, Judah would not have seen captivity. Instead, God would have protected her. But we must love the Lord our God above all others. He will not allow anything or anyone to take His place. It is only when we cultivate this kind of relationship with Him, that no matter where we find ourselves in life, we can call that place Jehovah-shammah.

MEDITATIONAL THOUGHT: *Our heart determines where God is*

Personal reflection: ______________________________

____

Prayer:

Dear Lord, Forgive me for the times I have been slack in my relationship with You. Or I have failed to place You first in my life. I hear and now incline my heart to You, so that whenever I call upon Your name, I will experience Your presence....Amen.

58. A Very Present Help

God is our refuge and strength, a very present help in trouble (Psalm 46:1)

Where is God when it hurts or when trouble is greatest? We sometimes ask ourselves this question because during those times, God can seem so far away. In fact, some Christians have become so bitter toward God during their tests, they have made Him their lifetime enemy. The truth is, the more difficult times are in our life, the closer He is to us.

The psalmist gives us three things that we find in God during troublesome times. One, He is our refuge. This is not a place where we reside forever. God has called us to fight on the battlefield. At times, however, and for a season, we need a refuge to shelter us from the storms of life. We find safety under the wings of God's protection. The enemy has no power over us in this place. As soldiers, at times we get wounded—physically, emotionally, or spiritually. The Lord is where we find healing, so we might return to the battle.

Two, God is our strength. This is good news because during the battles of life, our strength can fail us. God has given us but a measure of might. It was never His intent that we handle all the loads of life by ourselves. He designed us to need His strong arm. The Bible declares that His strength is perfected in our weakness. We may feel overwhelmed by the magnitude of the challenge at hand. It pales, however, in comparison to our God. One of the most valuable lessons we can learn is how to cast our cares upon Him in the time of trouble.

Three, God is our very present help. But how much do we believe this? The extent to which we do is directly related to the peace we have during times of difficulty. We know He is omnipotent. Nothing in life can come close to exhausting the resources that He can bring to bear on whatever it is that plagues us. True believers know this is true. The evidence of His wisdom and glory is seen in all of creation. But our knowing these things is not what gives us peace in times of trouble. To be sure, this peace can come only if we are confident that—in the time of trouble—this awesome God is very present and is actively working on our behalf.

MEDITATIONAL THOUGHT: *Where there is trouble, there is God*

Personal reflection: ______________________________

____

Prayer:

Dear Lord, I thank You for Your faithfulness. In times of trouble, others may forsake me, but I know I am never, never alone, because You are with me. In times of trouble, Your presence is my peace....Amen.

59. A Place for Meeting God

And there I will meet with thee, and I will commune with thee from above the mercy seat, from between the two cherubims which are upon the ark of the testimony… (Exodus 25:22)

We should safeguard our prayer time and our time of studying the Word of God. Through these, we experience intimate fellowship with God. This time of communing with Him should occur every day because that's how often we need His divine input into our lives. It pleases the Lord when we establish a place, say in our home, whereby we frequent His presence.

When God instructed Moses to build the tabernacle, He mandated a place for meeting with Him. This requirement was not driven by limited mobility on the part of God. He is omnipresent. But this place at which He would commune with the priests became sanctified. Similarly, when we establish a place for meeting with God, we are making a powerful statement. For one thing, it suggests that we value our time with Him.

This is not a call to legalism. We can and should be prayerful throughout our day. We don't have to resort to a particular place, as if God can hear us only from there. On the other hand, where a man's treasure is, there will his heart be also. When we seek His face, we must give Him our total attention. This is our moment to experience His presence. We need a place whereby we can leave this world as much as we can.

God honors such zeal for Him. It goes against the current grain of this society. We have become so casual with God because many people today want to experience Him on the fly. The church of today has gone quite far to accommodate this societal demand. But in the process of being flexible, we must never lose sight of the holiness of God. He will never succumb to the times. Casual worshippers will not experience spiritual intimacy with Him. They can get there only by loving Him with everything that is within them.

Jesus is our example. He understood the power of getting away from it all, and spending solitary time with God. Sometimes, He sent the multitudes away to be alone with the Father. At other times, He spent the whole night in prayer with God. This time with the Father was not at the expense of the vital work Jesus had come to do; rather, it was essential to its success. As He was in the world of His day, so let us be in our world today.

MEDITATIONAL THOUGHT: *Your most important meeting today is with God*

Personal reflection: ______________________________

____

Prayer:

Dear Lord, You are the source of my strength. You are the only one who can properly direct my life. I will pursue Your presence daily....Amen.

60. God Inhabits Our Praises

O thou that inhabitest the praises of Israel (Psalm 22:3)

Most of the things we offer God are for the direct benefit of others. When we bring monetary offerings to church, for instance, they are used to finance the operation of the ministry. God has no need of our money. When we serve Him, we do so by serving others, not Him. But when we offer praises to Him, they are for Him and Him alone. We may not always feel like praising Him. But He is always praiseworthy. Even when everything appears to be going terribly wrong for us, there are many reasons for which we should praise the Lord.

Praising God is not an option for the people of God. The Bible commands everything that has breath to praise Him. Then our failure to do so constitutes sin. Ironically, in some local churches this is not allowed. Praising Him openly is actually regarded as disruptive to their corporate worship service.

We miss out on an awesome blessing when we fail to praise God. He inhabits praises, the Bible says. That means when we praise Him, it ushers in His presence. Accordingly, local congregations that incorporate expressions of praise into their worship can enjoy a more intense presence of God. More importantly, when He shows up, He is never empty-handed. He comes ready, willing, and able to meet the needs of His people. Therein lies the power of praising the Lord.

We must be careful not to allow our praises to become conditional. This potential exists whenever we call ourselves judging the Lord's performance in our life. If we judge it to be below par, for instance, we may be tempted to refrain from praising Him. This is our way, we think, of protesting because He has not done something we were counting on Him to do. Or He has suffered us to be placed in a compromising situation.

First of all, who are we to judge God? How can the creature judge his Creator? Or, how can fallible men judge the infallible God to be unworthy of their praise? And what would be the effect of a man's verdict on God? To be sure, it would be nothing at all. But our refusal to praise Him would not be without effect upon us. While the sacrifice of praises can usher us into the presence of God as almost nothing else can, to conscientiously withhold the same is to deny ourselves access into His awesome presence—and everything He brings along to bless us.

MEDITATIONAL THOUGHT: *Let everything that has breath praise the Lord*

Personal reflection: ________________________________

____

Prayer:

Dear Lord, You are worthy of my praises. I will praise You daily. I know that where my praises are, there will Your presence be also....Amen.

61. With All My Heart

Thou shalt love the Lord thy God with all thy heart, and with all thy soul, and with all thy mind (Matthew 22:37)

Our concept of love is shaped by the eyes through which we view it. A woman can tell her husband she loves him very much and yet live guarded from him. Not because he has done anything to make her that way, but because someone else did in the past and those lingering wounds yet harbor mistrust. A man can claim to love his wife while not knowing what love is, having come from a dysfunctional home where he never saw love modeled before him.

So when we say we love God, what do we mean by that? Not that this question is without relevance. Asked what was the great commandment in the Law, Jesus said we must love God with all our heart, soul, and mind. That means we must love Him with everything that is in us.

To accomplish this end, we must cultivate our love for God daily. In doing so, we will find many corridors in our being, laden with hurdles to our quest that we must cross. For most of us, only a few of these hurdles take like forever to cross. Perhaps these were built by no fault of our own. But our obedience to the great commandment requires that we overcome these difficult areas. I am convinced of this one thing: God never calls us to do what He does not supply the resources to accomplish. He will certainly help us to love Him the way He commands us to.

Some Christians argue that their love for God is a private matter between them and the Lord. Even though others can't see the love they claim they have for God, they say He knows their heart. The latter point is certainly true. But our love for Him can never be the best kept secret in town because it becomes the fuel that drives the passion by which we serve Him. In practical terms, our love for God is reflected in the way we serve others, for that is how we serve Him.

The heart is a deceitful thing, tending to render a verdict of our self-assessment that bends toward the favorable. The only trustworthy standards we have, however, are the Word of God, the person of the Holy Spirit, and the life of Christ He modeled during His public ministry. Let us hear, be led by, and follow these.

MEDITATIONAL THOUGHT: *Our acts reveal our true heart*

Personal reflection: ________________________________

____

Prayer:

Dear God in heaven. You look on the heart and not the outer appearance. You know my every struggle to loving You completely. You know my conviction or the lack thereof to get there. My desire is to love You with all my heart....Amen.

62. Maintaining His Honor

But Jesus said unto them, A prophet is not without honor, but in his own country, and among his own kin, and in his own house (Mark 6:4)

The Lord shows us His goodness in abundance every single day. Over time, if we are not careful, we will no longer receive His blessings with appreciation. Rather, we will regard them as norms to be expected. If you are twenty years old, for instance, the Lord has blessed you to awaken at least the past 7300 days. It's easy to just expect Him to do the same on day 7301, 7302, and so on. Then you think it's no big deal, and you fail to thank Him for blessing you to awaken each morning.

Any kind of relationship is doomed to failure or to losing its vibrancy when those involved become too familiar with each other. Marriages stay strong when couples fail to take each other for granted. They do things to keep their appreciation for each other alive. Friendships are that way as well. Similarly, we must not become too familiar with the Lord. He had honor everywhere He went—except in His own hometown. There, they knew Him as one of the local guys. They knew His parents, brothers and sisters. To them, He could not possibly be the Messiah.

The problem with their attitude was that as they esteemed Him, so did they interact with Him. Because they did not regard Him as the Anointed One from God, they did not place their faith in Him as such. As a result, Jesus could do no mighty works in His own hometown.

Oftentimes, when a person first genuinely accepts Christ, she is extremely excited about her newfound relationship with Him and the glorious changes in her life. She is passionate about praying to the Lord and studying His Word. She underlines important points in her Bible, not wanting to miss out on anything God is saying through His Word. Like a sponge, she soaks up everything the preacher proclaims from the pulpit. With time, however, she gets familiar with many of the passages in the Bible. She has heard hundreds of sermons, and prayer begins to feel like no more than a ritual. With time, she is simply going through the religious motion.

This is very the process we must fight against with all that is in us. It is the enemy of our soul. We must labor to keep our relationship with the Lord vibrant each day, lest we take His person and His blessings for granted.

MEDITATIONAL THOUGHT: *Honor due is a function of the honoree*

Personal reflection: ______________________________

____

Prayer:

Dear Lord, You are so special to me. I place You above all others in my life. Let me never take for granted You or Your blessings. I want to experience You anew each day ....Amen.

63. Sanctified By His Word

Sanctify them through thy truth: thy word is truth (John 17:17)

To be effectively used by God, we must sanctify ourselves. That means we must set ourselves apart for Him. The call for us to do so has never been greater. We live in a world of chaos, uncertainty, and fear. The greatest need of humanity is to know the risen Savior. We must sanctify ourselves so we can be God's voice in the earth.

Intuitively, we don't know how to live for the Lord. His ways are too different from ours. What we regard as high and lofty can be abominable to Him. How blessed we are that He has given us the priceless treasure of His Word. Each day we study and open our heart to it, He speaks to us, correcting our wrong attitudes, challenging our commitment to holiness, rebuking us for indifference or nonchalance, confirming His love to us, and building us up in our faith.

When it comes to sanctification, our biggest enemy is not the devil or this world, but it is our own flesh. As long as we are clothed in it, it cries out to be pleased. No wonder Paul the apostle referred to his flesh as a body of death. You can see it raise its ugly head when you make up your mind to fast for several days—just as you have many times before. This time, however, you are having a rough time getting through day number two.

How about prayer time? A number of Christians have confessed to me that whenever they try praying more than 15 minutes, they run out of things to say, or they just fall asleep. Again, for Christians, this has nothing to do with the devil. The problem is with our flesh. When we become born again, our spirit is willing but our flesh is weak.

Because of this dynamic of the flesh, sanctification is not automatic for us. It will not come about merely as a result of how long we have been a Christian. In such passive mode of Christianity, the only thing we are assured of is a life of mediocrity in Christ. The Word of God is the instrument we must use, if we are to achieve sanctification. As we walk in His Word, it draws us closer to Him, and farther from ourselves and the ways of this world.

Christ is our perfect example. He came from heaven and lived on earth, modeling the sanctified life. The objective of the Word is that we follow His example so that as He was in the world so shall we be.

MEDITATIONAL THOUGHT: *We are in this world but not of it.*

Personal reflection: ______________________________

____

Prayer:

Dear God in heaven. The lure of this culture and the temptations of my flesh are ever present. I am committed to living for You in this ungodly world. I yield my will to Yours so that Your Word may prevail in every part of my life....Amen.

64. Our Weapons are not Carnal

For the weapons of our warfare are not carnal, but mighty through God to the pulling down of strongholds (2 Corinthians 10:4)

Because we belong to the Lord's army, our enemy the devil has declared all-out war against us. There is no level below which he will not go and no boundary he will not cross in his attempts to destroy us. By virtue of our enemy, this warfare cannot be conventional.

To get an idea of what we are up against, we have only to look at the United States. Right before our eyes, this great nation of ours seems to be drowning in a sea of calamity. The liberals blame the conservatives, and vice versa for our current state. None of our political machines, our military might, or technological advances are any match in stopping what we see happening before our very eyes. The main war we are in is not one of physical combat, nor is it technological, but it is spiritual.

So how can you and I stand in these final days? We must be strong in the Lord. This is not a moot point. Just because a person is a Christian does not mean he is strong in the Lord. Spiritual strength is not incidental to salvation. It is not a function of our time in the Lord. That is, it is not happenstance.

We can become strong in the Lord only if we learn to effectively use the tools He has provided us. The Bible refers to these collectively as the armor of God. We are enjoined to put on the entire armor, not just some of it. When we do, our enemy the devil is no match for us because then we become mighty—through God.

How we measure our strength is vital. If a person finds himself in a seemingly impossible situation, and he does not believe in God, he must assess his ability to overcome in terms of his own strength and no more. Accordingly, many people today find life daunting because they are no match for the challenge at hand. But the one whose strength is in the true and living God views things totally different. The person who knows how to pray, to walk by faith, and who believes that God empowers him to do the supernatural is totally unstoppable. There is no limit to where such a person believes he can go. The fuel that drives this conviction flows from how he measures his strength. Simply put, God is his strength.

MEDITATIONAL THOUGHT: *Not by power nor by might, but by my Spirit, says the Lord*

Personal reflection: ________________________________

____

Prayer:

Dear Lord, as I walk with You daily, I desire to live my life through Your power. Help me to put to death those stubborn works and ways of my flesh....Amen.

65. Self-Encouragement

Why are thou cast down, O my soul? and why are thou disquieted in me? hope thou in God….(Psalm 42:5)

Though born again, though Christ lives on the inside of us, though God uses us to do extraordinary things through the Holy Spirit, and though we encourage others along life's journey, we can get in the dumps at times. This dejection is often the result of external circumstances. But sometimes, we just feel down for reasons we can't explain. We shouldn't rely solely on external influences to pick us up. If we do, our emotional state will always be controlled by our environment. We must learn to minister to and to encourage ourselves at times. Note, I say learn.

Barring special circumstances such as medical depression and the like, only we have the power to keep our spirits down. Perhaps you have met a person who wanted to do just that—prolong the pity party. No matter what anybody tried to do to make him laugh and shake it off, he insisted on wallowing in his sorrow. As Christians, we need not visit such emotional state. Our hope is in the God of our salvation.

On the other hand, we maintain total control over how much we will allow the Lord to be the source of our hope. The Bible tells us to rejoice in the Lord always, for example. Why? Is it because Christians have nothing but good days? No, it is because no matter what life throws our way, God promises to deliver us from all of our afflictions.

Whenever we become downhearted, it is because we have failed to actively embrace the promises of God. They always point to victory. No matter how hopeless a situation seems, God promises that He will never leave nor forsake us. Why should we despair when He is in control and managing the affairs of our life? It's not enough for us to simply know these truths. They must be alive in our heart.

I continue to be mystified by the infirmities of our flesh. Sometimes, the least of things get the best of us. Even knowing that God is faithful, we sometimes fret while we wait on Him. Or we act out of haste, making a bad situation even worse. During such times, we should stem the madness, and challenge ourselves to focus on the God of our hope. He is the one who makes all things work together for our good.

MEDITATIONAL THOUGHT: *Timely words can come from us to ourselves*

Personal reflection: ______________________________

____

Prayer:

Dear Lord, forgive me for those times when I have allowed my circumstances to get the best of me. You are the source of all my hope. When my soul is cast down, I will encourage myself in You ....Amen.

66. Belief without Shame

For the Scripture saith, Whosoever believeth on him shall not be ashamed (Romans 10:11)

Faith requires trust. Oftentimes in life, trust is betrayed. This reality plays itself out many times when we go to make a purchase or to make an investment. Consider, for example, the experience of buying a used car. It's hard to know what you are getting. The salesman can make everything sound so good, when little do you know, he's pushing a lemon off on you.

When I was in my teens, a friend of mine who had saved a little money went to buy his first car. The purchase emptied his savings account, but he was so proud. I don't how he missed it, but the car had a bad front axle. After a few days of driving it, he could make turns in only one direction. That means every time he planned to go somewhere, he had to take a route that required him to turn only in that one direction. (I don't remember whether the car turned only right or only left.) Because the axle was bent, the front wheels were not in the true vertical position. They looked as if they would come off the car. Being young and kind of silly, we laughed to the point of hilarity every time we rode in that car. At times, a nearby driver would yell and say "your tire is coming off!"

Needless to say, my friend was very angry with the seller, not only because of the rotten deal, but also because the seller would not let him return the car and make a better selection. I won't tell you how my friend retaliated, but let's just say he made the dealer pay.

By contrast, God is always just in His dealings with us. He promises to save us, if we accept His Son who died on the cross for us. During our pilgrimage, we serve Him for a lifetime. We forsake serving ourselves and instead serve Him, invest money in the Kingdom on a regular basis, and grow spiritually by studying the Bible, praying, and working in the local church. During this journey, there are few visible signs that God is real or that He will make good on the salvation promise! We simply trust Him to do so.

This is not a natural process. No one in and of himself embarks on this journey. It is only by the divine work of the Holy Spirit in our heart that this giant leap of faith can be taken. And no partaker thereof will have shame for his end.

MEDITATIONAL THOUGHT: *God is not the author of gambles*

Personal reflection: ______________________________

____

Prayer:

Dear Lord, I thank You for my salvation experience. You are the faithful God who cannot lie. I totally trust You with my eternal end....Amen.

67. A Good Name

A good name is rather to be chosen than great riches, and loving favor rather than silver and gold (Proverbs 22:1)

Many people worship the dollar as king. It's not unusual to hear about some politician or preacher making the news by doing something unethical for monetary gain. This preoccupation for wealth makes many people vulnerable to con artists who lie in wait to deceive. Here is an idea: according to the Bible, a good name, a good reputation, far exceeds the value of riches and gold.

Think about our credit ratings. Potential lenders rely on these to determine the level of risk they will take if they lend us money. Our credit ratings are largely based on our record of payment to our creditors in the past. The premise is that a person's past performance is a good indicator of what his future performance will be. When a person has a bad name with creditors, though he may have the resources to repay the loan, he will probably need someone who has a better name than his to cosign on the loan in order to get it.

All Christians should value having a good name. We represent Christ and His Kingdom. We should do so in a way that brings glory to His name. It's more to it than simply saying we believe what the Scriptures say; that is, that a good name is to be preferred over riches. If we truly have that conviction we will labor toward that end just as those who love material wealth labor for it.

As for our actions, sometimes what we do is lawful but not expedient. So the Bible says we must abstain from all appearance of evil. For instance, there is absolutely nothing morally wrong about a

Christian going into a bar to witness to the lost for Christ. But in doing so, he must walk in wisdom, lest his good become evil spoken of. More importantly, he must be careful not to become a stumbling block to others by giving wrong impressions.

On the other hand, we must not become paranoid about doing the right thing. How many times did Jesus come under fire for the good He did just because the religious leaders did not understand where He was coming from? He did what He had to do, and so must we. But it would certainly be unwise for us to say we don't care what others say about us as long as we and God know the real deal. At all costs, we must labor to maintain a good name.

MEDITATIONAL THOUGHT: *Names don't make people; people make names*

Personal reflection: ______________________________

____

Prayer:

Dear Lord, help me to keep my eyes upon the right prize. No amount of money, power, or fame will I value above the honor of my name....Amen.

68. Faithful to All Generations

Thy faithfulness is unto all generations: thou hast established the earth, and it abideth (Psalm 119:90)

God didn't stop being faithful after biblical days. He is the same God to us that He was to Abraham, to David, and to Paul the apostle. This reality can be hard for us to see. We even ask ourselves, where is the God of the Bible? This question we raise because of the disparity we see between what God did in the lives of some of His servants during biblical times and what we observe as His acts today.

There are at least two possible explanations for the difference. One has to do with our relationship with God. Perhaps people like Abraham, David, and Paul walked more closely with God than we do today. It seems logical that the more intimate people are with God the more they would experience His glory. Another possible explanation may stem from His sovereignty. That is, perhaps He did the unique things He did among His servants during biblical times simply because He chose to at that time. But whatever the reason, the truth is that God's faithfulness to us in this current day is just as sure as it was to the patriarchs.

This must be our conviction if we are to have confidence in the Word of God. How unsettling it would be if we went to church, studied our Bible, believed in its teachings, but were unsure as to whether or not God still honored His Word as He did in days of old. Praise God, we have no such dilemma!

Our faith in God is the catalyst to our experiencing His faithfulness. This truth goes against the grain of natural thinking. We tend to shun expending effort unless we know we will benefit from the same. "Assure me of what You will do if I do thusly, and then I will do it," we say to God. Not in words, say we this, but in our heart or by our actions we do. But God demands that we walk by faith, believing that in the end we will see His faithfulness. Too, this is the only lifestyle whereby we can experience God as Christianity was meant to be.

This world has a dire need to see and hear of God's faithfulness in this generation. But how can this occur? It is by but one way. There must be a remnant that will give Him opportunity to prove Himself. That would be us.

MEDITATIONAL THOUGHT: *God's promises are surer than heaven and earth*

Personal reflection: ______________________________

____

Prayer:

God, I thank You that You have not forsaken or abandoned this generation. You are the same yesterday, today, and forever. Help me to walk with You in such a way that I am a living testimony of Your everlasting faithfulness....Amen.

69. The Sacrifice of Praise

By him therefore let us offer the sacrifice of praise to God continually, that is, the fruit of our lips giving thanks to his name (Hebrews 13:15)

We should praise God more often than we do. To deserve additional praise, He doesn't need to do anything else for us. If we were to magnify His name throughout each day for what He has done for us already, we would fail to do justice to His goodness.

Each and every day of our life is filled with God's praiseworthy deeds. This is true even during times of adversity—if only we could see beyond the present grief. Our test is not the story of our life. It is but a punctuation mark or a word or a sentence or perhaps a chapter of our lifelong journal. The Author and Finisher of our faith knows how to make all things work together for our good.

Oh, if we only knew the power of praise. This I say because of what happens on Saturday and Sunday mornings across America. Untold thousands come to the house of God to worship Him, but refuse to render praise. Do they not know that God inhabits the same (see Psalm 22:3)? He loves being in a place in which His people praise Him. This ushers us into His presence. What awesome privilege He has bestowed upon us, having made us priests unto Him. We can offer sacrifice to Him. Specifically, these are sacrifices of praise. They are uttered from our mouth but born in our heart.

Our passion for praising God or our failure to do so is a reflection of our relationship with Him. The stronger our connection with Him, the deeper the well is from which we draw the sacrifices of praise. This reservoir has been constructed of special material; namely, from a life of having experienced God's faithfulness over time. The flow of praise from this abode will not succumb to any dry season in life. It is only through this kind of relationship with God that we can offer to Him the sacrifice of praise—continually. That is the place to which He has called each of us. If we can only praise Him when things are good in life, in that regard, we are no better than those who don't know Him. We are priests unto Him, in good times and bad.

MEDITATIONAL THOUGHT: *A Christian void of praise is a priest who has no offering*

Personal reflection: ______________________________

____

Prayer:

Thank You for making me a priest unto You. My offering is the fruit of my lips. It is my desire to never withhold from You the sacrifice of praise ....Amen.

70. That Our Joy May be Full

And these things write we unto you, that your joy may be full (1 John 1:4)

Some people associate the Bible with legalism. Too many do's and don'ts, they say. Some even call the Bible old-fashioned. They say times have changed and the Bible can't possibly apply to our current culture. Some Bible-believing and -preaching ministers are labeled as mean-spirited or even religious bigots. But how many people associate the Word of God with fullness of joy? It is to this end that God moved upon holy men to write the Bible for us to have.

It can be argued that it is not necessary for us to fully obey the Bible in order to enter the Kingdom of heaven. That's because we are not saved by our works. Jesus died on the cross, and He has already paid the price to redeem us from sin. But our willingness to obey the Word of God is, among other things, a quality of life issue.

It is a wonder in and of itself as to how we even got our Bible. God used holy men to write it. Written by tens of writers, over a period of thousands of years, the Bible is a priceless resource of eternal truth without doctrinal error from heaven. In there we find counsel from the Creator of all things on every imaginable subject. Counsel that if we heed, we will never regret. Who's wiser than the One who created the heavens, the earth, and the minds of men? He knows the end from the beginning. For each of us, our purpose was determined before the foundation of the world began.

As we move toward the end of this age and the return of our Lord Jesus, I continue to be amazed at the accuracy of prophecies regarding the end times. As for the things that are happening in the world, such as a struggling world economy, horrendous natural disasters, and mounting tensions among the nations, we are not simply going through a cycle that comes and goes periodically, as some argue. Those of us with just a little biblical literacy can see Scriptures being fulfilled, and the staging for the end of this current age.

The fulfillment of the Scriptures testifies of God's wisdom and omniscience. If we heed them, His truths will navigate us through these chaotic times. Moreover, in God's Word we find great promises from Him. If we trust in Him, He will make good on every one. It is all to the intent that our joy might be full.

MEDITATIONAL THOUGHT: *Our potential for joy is measured by our appetite for truth.*

Personal reflection: ______________________________

____

Prayer:

Dear Lord, thank You for speaking to me through Your Word. You always know what's best for me. I will guard Your Words in my heart that I might know fullness of joy in my life....Amen.

71. All Things are Possible

Jesus said unto him, If thou canst believe, all things are possible to him that believeth (Mark 9:23)

"I have an impossible situation." How many times have you heard that said before? Sometimes the person makes this statement as a cliché because the challenge at hand is harder than average, but not overwhelming. At other times, however, it is because the answer to the problem is far beyond human grasp. In such cases, we must walk by faith, and not by sight.

There is no denying that life can be tough. Not for unbelievers only but also for believers in Christ. Not one time in Scripture, however, did Jesus or God tell anyone whom they had met that his situation was hopeless. That must be our conviction as well. There is always a way forward in Christ. This very statement triggers some important realities that are worth mentioning.

One is that some believers cannot receive this truth. Not necessarily because they doubt God's ability, but because of where they are spiritually. Babes in Christ can digest the milk of the Word but not the meat. They genuinely believe in Christ's redemptive work on the cross. But they have not reached the level of spiritual growth whereby they can operate in the more advanced levels of faith. As they grow spiritually, they will become more emboldened in their faith in God as well.

Another reality is that some Christians have preconceived notions and non-negotiable positions about what God's response should be on their behalf. The problem with such a view is that sometimes, their request and expectations are errant. What they believe God should do for them is not in the realm of possibilities. His very character and mode of operation won't allow Him to respond the way they think He should. Seeing no change that is compatible with their preconceived notions, they judge that God has not heard their prayers.

It behooves us, then, to qualify what Jesus means when He says that all things are possible to those who believe. This teaching is not a license to present our misguided requests to God and expect Him to grant them. The premise of all of Jesus' teachings is that we are operating consistently with Scripture. That is, when we come to Him in faith, asking according to His will, and placing our trust in Him, then all things are possible to us.

MEDITATIONAL THOUGHT: *Faith can take us where nothing else can*

Personal reflection: ________________________________

____

Prayer:

Dear Lord, I place my faith in you and not in myself. Forgive me for the times I have allowed challenges in my life to shake my faith. Help me to grow to the point that I can see that in You all things are possible....Amen.

72. The Miracle-Working God

The same came to Jesus by night, and said to him, Rabbi, we know that thou art a teacher come from God: for no man can do these miracles that thou doest, except God be with him (John 3:2)

Throughout the Old Testament period of the Bible, God worked miracles among His people. Jesus also performed miracles during His public ministry, as recorded in the New Testament. Furthermore, He taught His disciples that signs and wonders would follow those who believed the gospel He had charged them to preach.

The Lord did not work miracles just to show that He could. Rather, there were times during which God determined that heaven's proper response to the problem at hand was a miracle. And many people today need a miracle from God.

Consider the vast world of sicknesses and diseases. God has blessed us with a number of means to help us in the area of illnesses. There are medications that work wonders on certain ailments. Through research and more research, cures to some diseases are being found, albeit slowly. We have many skilled physicians who dedicate their lives to helping the sick to recover. But for some medical mysteries, none of the above can do much to help. These occasion the need for us to place our trust in the miracle-working power of God.

Throughout the Bible, there were many nations that did not worship the God of Abraham, Isaac, and Jacob. Instead, they worshipped other gods. Many of these false gods were graven or sculptured images. The people of those nations loyally followed these so-called gods. One way in which our God, the true and living God, distinguished Himself from all of the false gods was by the signs and wonders He worked among His people and before the heathens. Being the work of the hands of men, the other gods could not follow fashion. The same still holds today.

God showed Himself strong when He opened the Red Sea in the days of Moses so the people could cross over dry shod. In the days of Elijah the prophet, when the Israelites were confused as to who the true God was, He answered from heaven by fire to settle the debate. God has not changed over time. The book of the Acts of the Apostles is filled with accounts of God showing signs and wonders among the apostles, just as Jesus promised. The Lord still works miracles in the midst of His people.

MEDITATIONAL THOUGHT: *God has not ceased to be God*

Personal reflection: ______________________________

____

Prayer:

Dear Lord, You are the same yesterday, today and forevermore. I believe that You still work miracles today. When life tests me beyond the ability of natural means, I will trust You to bring me through….Amen.

73. Our Words Have Power

Death and life are in the power of the tongue: and they that love it shall eat the fruit thereof (Proverbs 18:21)

When I was a teen, I used to hear people say, "Sticks and stones may break my bones, but words cannot hurt me," or some variation of that. Now that I have gotten older, I know there's no truth to that saying. And the woman who suffered verbal abuse at the hands of her husband for a decade, telling her how worthless she was until she believed it herself, causing something to die inside her, she also knows the saying is not true.

More importantly, God says it is not true that words don't hurt. According to Him, we have the power to impart life to others via the things we say, or we can give them death. Both are at our disposal. We should choose to build up others and not to tear them down.

During Jesus' public ministry, He started a revolution. Wherever He went, throngs followed Him. Not because He was giving away free food or money. Rather, they followed Him for the Words He ministered to them. Whenever He opened His mouth, He imparted life to the people.

Years ago, a small congregation came together for an appreciation service for its pastor of over thirty years. As individuals stood up to make comments, they shared how that pastor had touched their lives. Most of it boiled down to his words: the inspiring sermons he preached, the lessons he taught, the counsel he gave, and the wise sayings he was known for. I left that appreciation gathering amazed at the many lives this preacher had touched through the power of his words.

We should create for us a similar legacy. When we are at a restaurant and the waitress serves us, for example, thank her while she serves us. Of course, she is only doing what she is being paid to do. But everybody wants to feel appreciated. Such a simple gesture can bless others.

If we adopt this practice, others will yearn to be in our presence. People love being around those who are positive. But who wants to be around a person who spews venom every time he opens his mouth? Furthermore, the things that leave our mouth reveal what resides in our heart. Or it's not possible to have a heart after the Lord and to love words of death at the same time.

MEDITATIONAL THOUGHT: *Plant and water good verbal seeds*

Personal reflection: ______________________________

____

Prayer:

Dear Lord, my heart is after Yours. I choose to use my tongue for good and not evil. I will speak words that encourage the discouraged, strengthen the weak, and embolden others for You....Amen.

74. The Earnest of Our Inheritance

Ye were sealed with that Holy Spirit of promise, Which is the earnest of our inheritance until the redemption of the purchased possession… (Ephesians 1:13b, 14a)

We are on a faith journey, headed for heaven and eternity. This experience begins when we accept Christ as our personal Savior. It ends when we meet Him at His return. But we have a taste of the Promise, even now. The Lord has given us the Holy Spirit as a token of our inheritance. In no way should this statement be taken to suggest that this is the sole purpose of the Holy Spirit. The Scriptures overflow with testimony regarding the person and works of the Holy Spirit.

When I bought my first house as a young man, the realtor told me I needed to give her $500 to move the process forward. She explained to me that, in effect, this earnest money was a token of the full down payment toward the house. This act gives the realtor a sense of commitment from the customer. It serves as a safeguard of sorts against those who will go and see a realtor and waste his or her time looking at houses they are not serious about buying. Putting some money up front suggests that you mean business. Similarly, every one of us who has a genuine relationship with the Lord has already received the Holy Spirit as earnest of what the Lord ultimately has in store for us.

The person of the Holy Spirit, living on the inside of us, enables us to experience a bit of heaven on earth. Christ, who will return one day in great glory to gather His church to Himself so that we might be with Him forever, lives in us even now through the Holy Spirit.

Having fellowship with the Holy Spirit in this life, we are virtually living in another world. We have been changed into a new creation in Christ. We have been called to walk with Him daily, and to pursue the things that are of the Spirit and not those that are of the flesh. Our mind should be heavenly focused. We are sojourners here just passing through.

This Christian lifestyle is a mystery to others in this world. They can't understand our driving passion. They can't understand why we are so sure about this God and heaven we cannot see. One reason is that we already have been given the earnest of our inheritance, and we are confident that God will make good on the rest.

MEDITATIONAL THOUGHT: *Though priceless, the Holy Spirit is a token!*

Personal reflection: ______________________________

____

Prayer:

Dear Lord, thank You for the Holy Spirit. Through Him Christ lives inside of me. Through Him I am ever reminded of the wonderful things You have in store for me in heaven....Amen.

75. Accepting Your Uniqueness

We, being many, are one body in Christ, and every one members one of another" (Romans 12:5)

Some people fall into the temptation of wanting to be like someone else. When I was a teen, there were a couple of pro athletes I wanted to be just like. I was not fascinated with looking like them, but I wanted to play their sport as well as they did. I also wanted to experience the success and notoriety they did. Several years ago, I came across several episodes on TV in which an everyday person got a complete makeover in an effort to look like his or her favorite star, if only for a day.

That same spirit oftentimes gets a hold of us in the ministry. I know of a pastor who changed the style of worship in his congregation because he believed this particular form of worship was a key element in the success of a well-known mega church that was watched by millions across the country. Apparently, the thinking was that if he modeled his ministry after this growing church, he would realize similar growth. Then there is the everyday church member who feels inadequate when he compares himself with fellow members who seem to be the total package.

But there is no other person on the face of this entire earth who can come close to being the person God made us to be. Why should we try being someone whom God did not make us to be? He did not create us an original only to live our lives trying to become a copy.

In several places, the Scriptures speak of the body of Christ in terms of the human body. Though there are millions of Christians throughout the earth, and though we have more denominations within Christendom than we can count, collectively, we are one body in Christ. Every

Christian plays an important role in that one body. There are no excess parts in the body. What each of us has to contribute makes a difference.

In 1979, while playing ball in the gym of my alma mater, I tore a cartilage in my right knee. I didn't know that was the problem until several months later. Before the doctor made the determination, all I knew was that I found myself walking bent-legged as much as a week at a time. Once my leg straightened out again, I thought all was well. But when I played on it, the pain and bent-leg experience started all over again. It amazed me that one torn cartilage could affect the performance of my entire body.

You see, that cartilage plays a specific role in my body. Nothing else inside of me can compensate for its failure to function. Nobody pays cartilage any attention until it fails to perform its God-given duty. The same goes for many of God's people. They don't play a visible role. Perhaps they get little or no thanks. But from the foundation of the world, God ordained that they would be a unique member of the body of Christ.

Perhaps the person I'm talking about is you. Know that you are uniquely you. Accept, and cooperate with your uniqueness. You bring an edifying effect to the body like no one else on God's earth can bring. Others may not appreciate you for who you are, but God does. In the end, that's what really counts.

MEDITATIONAL THOUGHT: *You are the first and last of your kind*

Personal reflection: ________________________________

____

Prayer:

Dear Lord, I am your wonderful handiwork. No one else is just like me. Help me to become the best rendition of the person You have made me to be.... Amen.

76. Our Fountain of Youth

"Though our outward man perish, yet the inward man is renewed day by day" (2 Corinthians 4:16).

Perhaps you have heard people talk about the so-called fountain of youth. It is a legendary spring that if a person were to partake of his youth would be restored. Of course, there is no such place, but the desire to perpetuate our youth lives on. Some people go on extreme diets, and pay exorbitant amounts of money for radical cosmetic surgeries and the like to try and stay young. Eventually, however, we will all lose the battle against the aging process.

But there is a way by which we who have accepted Christ as our Savior can remain young and vibrant throughout our days. For as we serve the Lord, He faithfully renews our strength.

Pastor Ray Tyson of the Emerald New Testament Church exemplifies this truth. He is a strong man of faith. The amazing thing about him is that as he has gotten older and his footsteps much shorter, his passion for God has not waned. That fire for God remains in his belly. Though his outward man has declined over time, yet his inward man remains as strong as ever.

"When I began preaching 40 years ago, one of the things that intimidated me was the thought of making good on my calling for the rest of my life," he told his congregation. "At the time, I was only 25 years old. What if after doing this for the next 10 years, I lost my passion for the gospel ministry? The problem was that I did not know about this spiritual truth that I am now sharing. I now know that when I yield my vessel to serve the Lord, and commit myself to enduring hardness as a good soldier, He restores me daily. I am not physically as young as I was back then. But the inner person that Christ made anew 40 years ago has not aged a bit! In fact, I am more committed to and passionate about Him today than I have ever been before."

OK, so Pastor Ray is somebody I made up, but I believe you get my drift.

Not every Christian experiences this daily renewal of his inner being. Rather, this mystery is reserved for those who commit themselves to faithfully serving the Lord, no matter what the challenges of life are. God's objective is that we minister in His strength and not our own. He faithfully supplies the wherewithal for us to do so. The virtue He puts on the inside of us is fresh and new each day, keeping us strong and vibrant all the days of our life.

MEDITATIONAL THOUGHT: *"The water that I shall give him shall be in him a well of water springing up into everlasting life"—Jesus Christ (John 4:14)*

Personal reflection: ______________________________

____

Prayer:

Dear Lord: You are the Source of my strength. When the rigor of the day has taken its toll on me, I will enter Your presence again. You restore my soul daily....Amen.

77. What Message Does Your Life Convey?

"Ye are our epistle written in our hearts, known and read of all men" (2 Corinthians 3:2)

"I'd rather see a sermon than hear one any day." In my early days as a Christian, I heard people say that. The point is that for some people, we are the only Bible they read. They draw their conclusions about Christianity from what they see in us. This tendency can yield a very wrong or distorted view of Christianity. Hence, we must be careful how we live our Christian lives.

It may seem unfair to us that, oftentimes, those outside of Christ frame their picture of Christianity based upon their observations of us. But that's a given we cannot change. Jesus had to cope with a similar situation during His public ministry. The Pharisees and other religious leaders kept His life under a magnifying glass. They tried to find fault with everything He did so as to discredit His ministry. But He gave them no occasion against the gospel. And though there may be a person or two who try to scrutinize us that way, they are not the subject of this devotion. Rather, it is the larger body of people who are not Christians, who have some curiosity about Christianity, and they are watching us who claim to be Christians to see what makes us a Christian.

This is not a call to perfection. Christians aren't literally perfect. They make mistakes, they do dumb things, and they can fail just like those don't know Christ as their Savior. But even in those instances, they should make amends in a way that reflects genuine Christianity. This is the kind of "lifestyle evangelism" that Christ calls His people to.

When our lives become living epistles that men can read and get the right message, regarding Christianity and the character of Christ, it will empower the work of the church. On the other hand, no matter how excellent the preaching is in the pulpits, and no matter how passionate our efforts are to win the lost, their effectiveness will be undermined by the way some Christians live among the very unbelievers we are trying to win. They hear what we are saying, but more importantly, they watch what we are doing.

MEDITATIONAL THOUGHT: *Some lives are read more often than books are*

Personal reflection: ______________________________

____

Prayer:

Dear Father, thank You for the change You have made in my life. I want to impact the lives of others who watch my life. Help me to live in such a way that my life portrays a picture of genuine Christianity ....Amen

78. Our Cloud of Witnesses

"Wherefore seeing we also are compassed about with so great a cloud of witnesses...let us run with patience the race that is set before us" (Hebrews 12:1)

I am reminded of a high school football game I once attended. It was a high-scoring game, and both teams played well. In the end the underdog team won. Later that day, I thought about the fans in the bleachers. They cheered their team on, and the players were feeding off the energy of the crowd.

We can do the same thing. The Bible says that we have a large crowd of witnesses. Many of them are mentioned in the book of Hebrews, chapter 11. They are men and women of faith who have gone before us. The biblical accounts of how they persevered and obtained a good report through their faith should encourage us during our Christian journey.

Interestingly, all of the witnesses mentioned in Hebrews, chapter 11, lived during the Old Testament era, but the book of Hebrews was written to New Testament believers. That's because God never changes. What we learn from the experiences of faithful men and women during the Old Testament should minister to us in our walk with God. If we take the position that we will read only the New Testament because we are living in the New Testament era, we will miss out on some valuable encouragement that is recorded in the Old Testament.

When we study the Bible and come across an account of a faithful servant of God who was tested in a way similar to the way we are being tested, and we see how the person endured to see God's faithfulness in the end, this should encourage us. It's as if the person is up in heaven cheering us on. Also, as we study the Bible and we see testimony upon testimony of how people of faith endured to obtain a good report, we should become more emboldened in our faith!

Everyone needs encouragement in his or her life. Though we have been born again and become new creations, we are still human, subject to human emotions. It behooves us to hang out among our awesome cloud of witnesses, such as Abraham, Moses, David, Joshua, etc. Their lives pour into ours as we study the Word of God faithfully. At the game, the high school teams fed off their fans in the bleachers. Today, let us feed off our witnesses in heaven.

MEDITATIONAL THOUGHT: *Following the footprints of faith, we dwell in good company*

Personal reflection: ________________________________

____

Prayer:

Dear Lord, as I study Your Word, may I hear the lives of your servants of old speaking to my life. You are the same God to me that You were to them. Their testimonies cheer me on as I run this Christian race....Amen.

79. God's Saving Power

For this cause I obtained mercy, that in me first Jesus Christ might show forth all longsuffering, for a pattern to them which should hereafter believe on him to life everlasting (1 Timothy 1:16)

God worked an awesome miracle in our life in order to save us from sin. If you don't believe that, just read some of the things the Bible says about our state before we got saved and the new creation we became afterward.

Another amazing thing about the Lord's salvation is the conditions under which He can save us. He can do so at any moment in any place. This is good news. Let's face it, some people will never come inside a place of worship. But that doesn't mean God can't reach them. He can save sinners in bars, upon a hospital bed, in prisons, you name it.

Paul the apostle is an excellent example of God's saving power. Before becoming a Christian, Paul was one of the most evil men on earth. He persecuted the church in his day. As he headed for Damascus to persecute the Christians, however, he met the Lord Jesus Christ as his Savior.

Saul of Tarsus was not seeking the Lord when he met Him. He was up to no good. But God apprehended him for the Kingdom! He was no longer the mean, religious man who went about hating Christians. He became a new creation. He became known as Paul the apostle, and he was the greatest of the Lord's servants recorded in the New Testament.

Paul's salvation experience is recorded in the Scriptures as an example of God's saving power that is available to all. If He can easily save a deceived and blasphemous man like Saul, it is but a light thing for Him to save any sinner who comes to Him. This truth must become our personal conviction.

Why? Because what we believe drives what we do. If we believe a person can become so wicked and lost that even God can't save him or her, our tendency will be to write the person off. Some individuals actually believe that about themselves—that they are so lost that even God can't deliver their soul. Again, it is but a light thing for God to save them.

Because of the persecution the church at Jerusalem experienced at the hand of Saul, we can logically assume that the believers were crying out to God. And on Saul's way to Damascus, God remembered their prayers and apprehended Saul. Maybe there is a lost person in your life whom you have given up on. Continue to pray and believe God. One day He will remember your prayers. And it is but a light thing for Him to save your loved one(s).

MEDITATIONAL THOUGHT: *No unbeliever who truly meets Christ survives the meeting*

Personal reflection: ______________________________

____

Prayer:

Dear God, I truly thank You for saving me. I want others to experience Your awesome saving power. Increase my passion for lost relatives and friends….Amen.

80. Discovering the Ways of God

How unsearchable are his judgments, and his ways past finding out! (Romans 11:33)

To make any system work for you, you must first understand how that system works. Similarly, in order for Kingdom principles to work for us, we must first understand how they work. Too often, Christians interact with God based on their ill-conceived notions about Him, and they are disheartened with the results they get. The problem is that when we deal with God we must do so in a manner consistent with His ways.

But we don't intuitively know the ways of God. We can't go on an expedition to discover His ways, as NASA does space explorations to learn about space and the universe. The only things we know about the ways of God are those which He reveals to us in His Word. We have no other means of discovering His ways.

Note, I did not say we cannot discover some of God's works, such as through archaeology. Scientists have found many relics that confirm certain accounts in the Bible. But what I am talking about are the ways of God; His modus operandi.

In the accounts of the gospel, Jesus often introduces His teachings by saying, "The Kingdom of heaven is like…." When He does that, He is revealing to us a Kingdom principle and how it operates. Why are these teachings important? Because, again, in order for us to make Kingdom principles work for us, we must first understand how those principles work. The more we study the Bible, the more we learn the ways of God and how the principles of His Kingdom work. The better we learn them, the more we can make them work for us.

The dilemma of a new convert is that upon accepting the Lord Jesus Christ, he knows little if anything about the ways of God. Not knowing how to interact with God, he simply does what he knows. Some tend to reduce God to a man because human relationships are all they have known. But God is not a man. What works for us in dealing with our neighbor or a colleague will not work with God. That's why we must study our Bible. It is His gift to us. He inspired holy men to write it so we could have it. It is our only means of discovering His ways. This is important because God always deals with us in a manner that is consistent with His ways.

MEDITATIONAL THOUGHT: *As the heavens are higher than the earth, so are God's ways higher than ours*

Personal reflection: ______________________________

____

Prayer:

Dear God, thank You for revealing Your ways to me in the Scriptures. As I learn Your ways, help me to abandon my own. I want others to see Your character in my life....Amen.

81. Priests Unto God

Ye also, as lively stones, are built up a spiritual house, a holy priesthood, to offer up spiritual sacrifices….(1 Peter 2:5)

As true believers, we are priests to the Lord. This honor is not the product of our works in the Lord. Our societal status has no place in this matter. The ceremonial decrees of men can't bestow this office. It is solely through Christ's redemptive work on the cross that we have been made priests to God.

Our offerings are not animals and their blood as was the case in the Old Testament; rather, they are spiritual sacrifices—a song to Him, praises to His name, the sharing of a testimony on His behalf, etc.

These sacrifices are not occasioned by the formal gatherings of men and women, such as worship in the house of God. If that were the extent of our priestly activity, we would be partakers of no more than ritualism. We are called, rather, to know the God whom we serve as priests so that our offerings stem from our heart. In turn, we make any place before which we stand a altar of our sacrifice.

It should not be burdensome for us to commit ourselves to becoming faithful priests to the Lord. Let the redeemed of the Lord say so. Our God has been extremely good to us. We can't tell the number of His many blessings. Let us count Him worthy of our coming before Him throughout each day and offering Him spiritual sacrifices. Even when we do so, our offerings are weighed and found wanting.

Lest we trivialize our calling to this priesthood, we dare not forget the object of our sacrifices. He is the holy and living God. Polluted offerings affront His person. This is not a call to perfection or infallibility but to reverence and purity of heart. God does not look on the outward appearance. He sees the heart behind our offerings. If no pretense is found there, our offerings become acceptable sacrifices, ascending before Him as a sweet-smelling fragrance.

What an awesome privilege we have been granted in this New Testament era. Only those from the house of Levi could be priests in the Old Testament. God chose them to make offerings on behalf of the people, thereby placing them at the mercy of this select group. But through Christ's work on the cross, we all have been granted access to offer to God on our own behalf!

MEDITATIONAL THOUGHT: *Spiritual sacrifices move the heavens*

Personal reflection: ________________________________

____

Prayer:

Dear Lord, I thank You for my priesthood. You deserve the best of my offerings. May the deeds of my day, the words of my mouth, and the meditations of my heart be acceptable to You.... Amen.

82. Hallowed be Thy Name

After this manner therefore pray ye: Our Father which art in heaven, Hallowed by thy name (Matthew 6:9)

The "guy upstairs"; the "big guy"; sometimes you may hear a person refer to God by names such as these. This should never be done. His name is worthy of veneration. He is exalted above all nicknames.

To underscore this point, Jesus taught that when we pray we should say, "Hallowed be thy name." Now we all know the person of God is holy. But Jesus says God's very name is holy! That means His name has been set apart from and above all that is common. Though we say these words of Jesus in our prayer to God, how much do we think about the implications of those words?

We are living in a time in which we hear atheists and comedians on TV rail against God for fun or out of anger. They all but dare Him to retaliate. We must not let this blatant irreverence toward God infect us. If we do no more than use His name in vain, it behooves us to repent.

This idea of one's name demanding respect is not a novel one. For over 25 years, I have worked as an engineer at a government agency. Oftentimes, we receive new technical criteria and engineering guidance to implement. It is not unusual for us to receive this guidance at first in draft form so those interested can comment on what is being proposed. But when this criteria or guidance becomes official, we often receive it under the signature of at least one general of the U. S. Armed Forces. Once the document is so signed, we regard it as the law of our technical world. It is not an option for any of us to disobey the instructions of the general.

He is hundreds of miles away from our office. He doesn't have to show his face. All we need is to see his name on the signature line, and we take the orders and run with them. If the name of a mortal man can carry so much authority for respect, how much more so should we revere the name of our God?

But what is His name that we should hallow it? The Bible attributes a number of names to God. Any of those names is His name. So whether we address Him as God, our Father, Jehovah-jireh, etc., the mandate is the same—hallowed be His name.

MEDITATIONAL THOUGHT: *"You shall not take the name of the Lord your God in vain"*

Personal reflection: ________________________________

____

Prayer:

Dear Lord, I reverence Your name. I will set it above all others. I will not engage Your name in foolish conversation....Amen.

83. Service Without Love

If I give all I possess to the poor and surrender my body to the flames, but have not love, I gain nothing (1 Corinthians 13:3, NIV)

What do we mean when we say we are servants of God? To serve someone, we must be equipped to minister to a need that the person has. God is never such a person. He is Creator of the heavens, the earth, the seas, and everything in them. So how do we serve a God who owns everything and needs nothing? We can do so only by serving others.

The needs of the family of God and humanity at large are astounding. No shortage of opportunities exists for us to get involved in serving God through serving others. In fact, the needs around us are so great that they can seem overwhelming at times. But God has adequately equipped us for such a time as this.

More important than the good deeds we do is the motivation behind our actions. In the eyes of God, love must always be the fuel that drives our acts of serving others. He does not look on our outward performance but on our heart.

The way the world views service and giving of one's resources greatly differs from God's way of thinking. In the world, a large business can contribute a substantial financial contribution to a highly visible, humanitarian cause solely because it's good publicity for the company. No one cares about where the company's heart is relative to the cause at hand. Good will come out of its deed, and that's the bottom line. But when Christians give or serve and love is not the motive, in the eyes of God, it profits nothing!

This verdict is no condemnation on the service that we render. Rather, it underscores God's commandment for His people to walk in love. Even more powerful than the things we do is the love that we walk in. This love conveys something profound about the One who lives on the inside of us. The world should know that we are His disciples, not by the things we do but by the love we show each other.

Our being Christians is no guarantee that our motive(s) for serving others is always right. We still have the capacity to walk in the flesh or in the Spirit. Furthermore, these two entities of our being seldom have the same agenda. It behooves us then to examine the motivation behind our deeds. Let us make sure that love is always in the driver's seat.

MEDITATIONAL THOUGHT: *Right actions plus wrong motives equals nothing to God*

Personal reflection: ________________________________

____

Prayer:

Dear Lord, thank You for Your love You have placed on the inside of me. Rule in my heart as I serve others. I want them to see Your love shining through my life….Amen.

84. Infinite Understanding

Great is our Lord, and of great power:
his understanding is infinite (Psalm 147:5)

Life is a mystery to us. We can't understand why many things are as they are. Why is it, for instance, that so many innocent babes in certain parts of the world are born into incredibly horrible conditions? When horrific natural disasters occur, some people are prompted to ask, how can a loving God allow such an awful event to occur?

Then there are those seasons of personal tragedy. We are all tested at one time or another. This is true for the just as well as the unjust. Neither the Christian, the non-Christian, or the atheist is exempt from personal trials. And there is no guarantee from heaven that if you live for God and try to please Him each day of your life that you will see less adversity than someone who doesn't.

OK, what's happening? How do we make sense of these apparent contradictions? Where is God in all of this?

We might be tempted to conclude that He is not the Judge of all the earth. Or that He can't relate to the world we live in or to the situations we find ourselves in. The truth is that He totally understands each one of His children. He has a perfect plan for their lives. His hand is never slack in bringing it to pass.

There is no area or dimension of our life that God does not fully understand. Ironically, the fact that our understanding pales in comparison to His is what causes us to misread Him. That's why the Bible says we must walk by faith and not by sight.

When we pray and seek God's face, He understands our situation better than we do. Yes, we know the pain and desperation we feel. We know what we think needs to be done to solve the problem at hand, and that we are not shy about expressing to Him.

But only God perfectly knows the plan He has for our life, and how the matter at hand fits into that plan. Only He knows how to make all things work together for our good. He knows when the do-or-die date that we imagine is simply borne of our spiritual nearsightedness. And He knows what needs to be done to sustain us until He turns our captivity. There is not one minor detail of any situation in our life that He fails to fully understand during His dealings with us.

MEDITATIONAL THOUGHT: *The better the understanding the more appropriate the response*

Personal reflection: ________________________________

____

Prayer:

Dear Lord, You always understand my case better than I do. You always know what's best for me. Even when it's not apparent, You are working on my behalf. I trust You with my personal trials....Amen.

85. The Prayers of the Saints

And another angel came and stood at the altar, having a golden censer; and there was given unto him much incense, that he should offer it with the prayers of all saints upon the golden altar which was before the throne (Rev. 8:3)

"O what peace we often forfeit. O what needless pain we bear. All because we do not carry everything to God in prayer." These words are taken from an old and beloved hymn entitled, "What a Friend We Have in Jesus." But the lyrics are more than mere words we sing. They tell a truth that we sometimes fall victim to.

God cares so much for us. He wants to provide for our every need. He wants to give us the desires of our heart, and to aid us in our decision-making in life. But we will miss out on this abundant grace if we fail to carry everything to Him in prayer.

Prayer to God does not require us to talk like a theologian. At times we may feel so burdened that we can't find the right words to say to Him in prayer. But if He were to open our eyes and let us see in the spirit how He regards our prayers when we pray to Him, we would be amazed. When we walk in obedience to Him, our prayers are pleasant to Him. They are like a sweet-smelling fragrance ascending to His nostrils.

Our prayers please God this way because they invite Him to be a part of our affairs. They release Him to show His good pleasure toward us. Like an earthly father who cherishes the opportunity to love and to provide for his children, our heavenly Father loves it when we petition Him through prayer and afford Him the opportunity to show His fatherly love toward us.

This benefit we owe to Christ for His redemptive work on the cross. It is through His obedience that we have been made righteous. When we pray, God does not deal with us according to our own righteousness. He sees us clothed in His righteousness because of Christ. It is only through this sacrificial work of Christ that our prayers can be made a sweet-smelling sacrifice to a holy God.

We should strive to develop a consistent prayer life. This discipline yields awesome returns on our investment of time with the Father. As the hymnologist asked, why should we forfeit peace? Why do we bear needless pain? Our heavenly Father sits ready, willing, and able to answer our prayers.

MEDITATIONAL THOUGHT: *Prayer gives us daily access to heaven*

Personal reflection: ______________________________

____

Prayer:

Dear Lord, I come to You in the name of Jesus. It is by His blood that I have been made to be the righteous. Whenever I pray, I am confident that You desire to show your good pleasure toward me....Amen

86. Christ's Commitment to His Church

Husbands, love your wives, even as Christ also loved the church, and gave himself for it (Ephesians 5:25)

Love requires commitment, and commitment requires giving of oneself. Jesus made the most priceless commitment to His Church when He gave His very life for her. Be it known to all that He will now give and do whatever it takes to protect His investment. How can the Church do anything but win?

The Bible refers to the Christian Church as Christ's bride. This analogy underscores the relationship between the two. Like a marriage ordained in heaven, the two have become one, never to be two again. Each day, Christ labors faithfully to minister His endless love to His bride.

That His bride is not without shortcomings is an understatement. In many areas she fails, or even refuses to submit to her Head, who is Christ. It would be fair to call the relationship between Christ and His bride extremely one-sided.

But His love for His Church is unconditional. What she is or what she is not has no bearing on His devotion to her. He sees her not as she is but as she shall be. When the two meet at His coming, the Church will be more stunning than a bride adorned for her husband. She will be without blemish.

Viewing the Church in her current state, we may find it hard to believe that her end will be so glorious. Some of her prominent leaders have occasioned reproach. Division within has spawned many splinter groups causing her to weaken and to become divided against herself. Some elements of society have vowed to silence her voice.

Her end, however, will be glorious and victorious. This proclamation speaks not to the Church's commitment to Christ but of His commitment to the Church.

But what is the Church? It is not a building. It's not an organization. The Church is the body of Christians collectively. Christ is committed to everyone who belongs to the Church. He has begun a good work in us, and He will finish that work if we allow Him to.

Commitment in a relationship breeds security. Christ made a serious commitment to us by giving Himself at Calvary in our stead. No matter where we currently are in our relationship with Him, let us be confident that He is totally committed to our completeness in Him.

MEDITATIONAL THOUGHT: *True love gives more than it demands*

Personal reflection: ________________________________

____

Prayer:

Dear Lord, thank You for Your Son who loved me so much that He gave Himself for me. In due season, I will see Him face to face. No matter how contrary my life may seem at times, I will not doubt Your undying love for me....Amen.

87. Perfected Forever

For by one offering he hath perfected forever them that are sanctified (Hebrews 10:14)

As Jesus hung on the cross, just before He commended His Spirit to God and died He said, "It is finished." His words signified that everything necessary to redeem us from sin had been completed on Calvary. This provision did not apply only to those who lived during Jesus' public ministry but also to all generations that would follow.

Some may ask the question, how can it be that Jesus died on the cross nearly 2000 years ago, and His redemptive work applies to us as well? Really, this is but a light thing for God. He is the same God who at the beginning of creation, placed within the earth water and resources ample to sustain all generations to follow. If He can provide sustenance for all generations at one point in time, why can't He also provide redemption for all generations through the death of His Son?

Equally important, Jesus' death makes us complete forever. This declaration should not be taken to mean that after we accept His death on the cross as adequate payment for our sins, we never miss the mark. Rather, unlike during the Old Testament era during which the priests had to offer sin offerings daily for the sins of the people, Christ's death on the cross requires no additional work. It is sufficient to keep us perfectly right with God throughout our time on this earth. When we sin, we can ask God for forgiveness on the authority of what Christ did on the cross for us. And God will grant it, thereby cleansing us from all unrighteousness!

God's will is that we walk through this life, being in the world as Christ was when He walked the earth. The truth is that no one has ever fully succeeded in doing so. Hence, we cannot be saved by our own deeds but only by Christ's obedience to death on the cross.

The day will come when all of us must meet the Lord. That will be a most dreadful day for many. But we who have placed our faith in Christ's work on the cross can face that day with boldness. Clothed in His righteousness, we will stand before the Lord, holy and just.

MEDITATIONAL THOUGHT: *Perfection is heaven's minimum requirement.*

Personal reflection: ________________________________

____

Prayer:

Dear Lord, thank You for saving my soul. I rejoice that I don't have to stand in my own sufficiency. My sufficiency lies solely in Christ. Through Him, I am confident of my eternal security….Amen.

88. God is Not a Man

God is not a man, that he should lie; neither the son of man, that he should repent (Numbers 23:19)

Surely none of us would call God a man. That would be outright blasphemous. It would be like saying He has limitations or that He is fallible or that He lies at times, and so on. For all of these shortcomings belong to all human beings.

Sometimes we are guilty of effectively regarding God as a man. This happens whenever we feel that just because we can't see how He can solve our problem, He must not be able to do so. It's as if we are saying God is limited in what He can do. But we must never view His ability through the eyes of men. He is omnipotent. He has ways at His disposal that we know not of.

Our concept of God is defined by our faith in Him. This in turn determines how we view the challenges we face in life. That is, the deeper our faith in God becomes, the less we will be moved by the hand that life deals us.

For example, our God is greater than any sickness that can invade our bodies. We should not simply lie down and wait to die because we have been diagnosed with a fatal disease. We should pray to God and truly believe what the Bible teaches about His hearing and answering the prayers of His children. No situation we face in life can change that truth. He is not a mere man. He still works miracles in these last days. He is the same God today that He was in days of old.

The Bible is filled with His promises. These He has given us to comfort, edify, and to guide us. It is vitally important that when we hear or read the Word of God that we bear in mind the Author of the same. No other collection of literary works can compare to the Bible. All others are the products of mere mortals. This places the Word of God in a class all by itself. Let us embrace it that way.

We can trust what God says. We can build our life on His promises. He is not a man. He never lies. He never flip flops. His counsel never fails. He is never at a loss as to what to do about our personal case. Through Him we are more than conquerors.

MEDITATIONAL THOUGHT: *What's impossible for men is easy for God*

Personal reflection: ______________________________

____

Prayer:

Dear Lord, You are the Rock of my salvation. All other ground is sinking sand. You are the God of no limitations. Help me to trust You with my life completely....Amen.

89. Grace Abounds More

Moreover the law entered, that the offense might abound. But where sin abounded, grace did much more abound (Romans 5:20)

None of us can be justified by obeying God's commandments. The truth is that He did not give us His many commandments in the Bible to make us right with Him. One intent of the Law is to show us how much of a wretch we are. The Law shows us how badly we need a Savior. The good news is that no matter how awful a person sees himself as being when he looks in the mirror of the Law, the grace of God is always more than enough to save the lost.

This amazing grace does not cease to exist upon our salvation. If it did, none of us would see the pleasant face of our Lord on the other side. For we are not literally perfect upon salvation, though legally we are. At times we may feel far from God. Studying His Word through which He conveys to us His holiness and His will for our lives, we know at times we don't measure up. Hence, the grace of God is not an option but a must for us.

Although we should pray to God about everything, He sometimes does not respond the way we ask Him to. Instead of delivering us, He may give us grace to go through the test. We should see this way of God as a blessing. Just think about how our life would be if He removed every test, and we never had to endure any hardship. But at times He allows us to be tested so we can learn more about trusting Him. The anchor for our soul comes through knowing that whenever God chooses to allow us to go through a difficult situation, His grace will be more than enough to get us through it.

Let us not be deceived about the matter of grace. That God gives us grace in abundance does not trump His demand for us to live holy lives. This is His due. Having been bought with the blood of Christ, we belong to God. He expects nothing less than total surrender from us. In the very end, we will give account to Him for our stewardship while on this earth. In our earnest desire to give Him the best version of ourselves, we will fail many times along the way. In that we don't despair, but in this we are confident: where shortcomings abound, grace abounds more.

MEDITATIONAL THOUGHT: *Living by grace and living by the Law are mutually exclusive*

Personal reflection: ______________________________

____

Prayer:

Dear Lord, You are the God of my salvation. I will boast that my salvation is already settled in the heavens. Not because of my works, but because of Your grace….Amen.

90. King of Kings and Lord of Lords

And he hath on his vesture and on his thigh a name written, KING OF KINGS, AND LORD OF LORDS (Rev. 19:16)

The Second Coming of Christ will signify the end of this present earth. Then shall the will of God be done on earth as it is in heaven. At His coming, all the earth will acknowledge Christ as King of kings and Lord of lords.

King of kings because He will reign, and His Kingdom will be the last one ever established. It will be a Kingdom without end. The kingdoms of this world will give way to the Lord's glorious Kingdom. He will reign in righteousness. How refreshing that will be. No more corruption in government. No more partisan rhetoric. No more death, pain, and sorrow.

Lord of lords because at His coming, all of the mighty of the earth will bow before Him and acknowledge Him as Lord of all the earth. This was God's decree before the foundation of the world. As we see around us, however, many have not taken this divine mandate to heart. God has given the world a space for repentance. Ultimately, His desire will prevail.

Jesus' return shall not be as His birth was. First He came to be the Savior of the world and the Lamb of God who bore our sins. But the second time, He will judge the devil and his angels, the anti-Christ and their human followers, after which He will reign forever.

We who keep the faith until the end will forever be with Christ. We will live in His eternal Kingdom. He will be our King and Lord, ruling with the scepter of righteousness. All who truly know the Christ as their Savior have this testimony.

The devil aims to avert our destiny. To him, all is fair in war. By any means necessary, he would have us to renounce our faith and our hope in Christ. All of his works are aimed at this one objective.

But they pale in comparison to the joy that awaits us at the victorious coming of our Lord. What the Scriptures reveal is but a hint to what God has in store for us. However profound they are, such revelations do not come close to conveying our glorious end. It is worth enduring whatever tests the present life throws at us.

MEDITATIONAL THOUGHT: Our future is already history.

Personal reflection: ________________________________

____

Prayer:

Dear Lord, I thank You in advance for my glorious end. I will not despair as the world does. For this troubled earth is not my home. Christ has gone to prepare a perfect place for me. He will personally come to usher me there....Amen.

Keep the Fire Burning

Throughout this book, you have been consistently doing four things: reading a Bible verse and a short commentary, meditating on a relevant point, personally reflecting, and praying the essence of the devotion back to God. In closing, I want to encourage you to incorporate the latter part, praying the Word of God back to Him, into your daily personal Bible study from this day forward. The benefit is that you will experience transforming moments with God for a lifetime.

I carefully selected the verses that I used in this book. But they were mainly based on the subjects I deemed important to address. The truth is that the process you have been using to work through each of the devotions in this book can be applied to any and every chapter of the Bible.

Let me give you a couple of examples. Some time prior to my writing these closing words, I was studying the book of Jeremiah. In chapter one of that book, God said these words to Jeremiah: "Today I have made you a fortified city, an iron pillar and a bronze wall to stand against the whole land—against the kings of Judah, its officials, its priests and the people of the land. They will fight against you but will not overcome you, for I am with you and will rescue you," declares the Lord (Jeremiah 1:18-19, NIV).

After reading the chapter, I thought about what God had said to Jeremiah. Being a preacher myself, I began to talk to the Lord about the passage. I said something like this: "Lord, I thank You that as a preacher of the gospel, I never have to fear men. You have made me like a fortified city. When opposition arises, You are with me, my battles belong to You, and You always cause me to triumph…."

There was nothing I read in the book of Jeremiah I had not read many times before. My prayer as a result of reading chapter 1 of the book of Jeremiah was not based on any new revelation. But praying the Word back to God stirs up the truths in me that over time can become dormant. Doing this helps to keep my faith in God vibrant.

I believe that too many Christians passively read the Bible. Sometimes, they want to read as much as they can in as little time as possible. Or perhaps they are trying to put the time in to read through the Bible in one year. But God does not want us to merely read the Bible. He wants us to experience its biblical truths. That requires us to interact with God about what we hear Him saying to us through His Word.

OK, let's try another example, one that's more generic. After Jesus was crucified, the Bible says on the first day of the week that God raised Him from the dead. As Mary Magdalene and the other Mary sat by the tomb, the angel said: "I know that you seek Jesus, which was crucified. He is not here: for he is risen, as he said" (Matthew 28:5b-6a).

When I recently read that, I thought about how Jesus told the disciples beforehand that He would be crucified, and afterward He would be raised from the dead. He was confident that if He committed His Spirit into the hands of God that the Father would raise Him again from the dead. Think about it; if God did not come through, Christ would be forever dead! So I began to thank God for His faithfulness. I told Him that I too trusted Him with my life, and that I knew when I die, He would raise me up at the return of His Son….

I think you get my point based on the two examples above and based on what you have been doing throughout this book. It's important for you to know that there is no one correct response to God during your personal Bible study. Well, yes there is. The correct response to God is based on what you hear Him saying to you through the portion of the Bible you are studying. There is also no minimum time you must talk to God about what He is talking to You about.

Again, this can be done with any chapter in the Bible. I have been practicing this discipline for many years, and I can truly say that it has revolutionized the time I spend in the Word of God. It is my prayer that you will incorporate this discipline into your life, and that through it you will experience transforming moments with God for a lifetime.

Finally, I want to thank each and every one of you who supported me through buying this book. I want to especially thank those of you who faithfully used the book. May the grace of our Lord Jesus, the love of God, and the communion of the Holy Spirit be with you.

Blessings,
Frank King